The West Street Ambassadors

Troy, Ohio's WW II Junior Girls
Canteen for Servicemen

Scott D. Trostel

© Copyright 2006 Scott D. Trostel

All rights reserved. No part of this book may be reproduced in any form or by any means including electronic, photocopying, or recording or by any information storage or retrieval system, without written permission.

Printed in the United States of America

First printing
2 3 4 5 6 7 8 9

Library of Congress Cataloging-In-Publication Data

Trostel, Scott D.
  The West Street ambassadors : Troy, Ohio's WW II Junior Girls Canteen for servicemen / .
     p. cm.
Includes bibliographical references.
  ISBN-13: 978-0-925436-53-5
  ISBN-10: 0-925436-53-4
1. Junior Girls Canteen (Troy, Ohio) 2. World War, 1939-1945—Ohio—Troy. 3. World War, 1939-1945—War work—Ohio—Troy. 4. World War, 1939-1945—Women—Ohio—Troy. 5. World War, 1939-1945—Children—Ohio—Troy. 6. Canteens (Establishments)—Ohio—Troy. I. Title.
  D769.85.O31T767 2006
  940.54'77977148—dc22

2006018200

**CAM-TECH PUBLISHING
P.O. BOX 341
FLETCHER, OHIO 45326-0341**

ISBN No. 0-925436-53-4

Preface

From mid-1943 to early 1946, nearly 40 of Troy's young ladies, and their mothers, friends and neighbors, operated a community-based free canteen for the soldiers in WWII. Their enduring purpose was to lighten a weary serviceman's burden with food, drink and cheery words.

The all-volunteer Junior Girls Canteen provided nearly three years of dedicated service to over 600,000 soldiers on all passing trains. The good it did positively impacted Troy and the nation for many years.

Untold thousands of boys in all parts of America and in all walks of life were provided sandwiches, pecan pies, cookies, coffee, magazines and friendly smiles as their trains paused at the Baltimore & Ohio Railroad station on West Street in Troy. The volunteers gave up their free time, a little sleep and a proper meal for compassionate service to strangers.

Residents of Troy and communities in six counties were united by a single cause in support of those girls efforts. The community contributed in many ways to the canteen's success. It was a success because of the desire to serve strangers in uniform at trackside. The Canteen Girls served troops on passenger trains, entire Troop Trains, new recruits and returning veterans. They were witnesses to the cost of war in serving the wounded veterans on Hospital Trains. They served every train no matter the hour, in summer's heat and some of the worst winter weather in 100 years.

Mrs. Mary Tooley, the Canteen manager, and her capable assistants overcame many difficulties which would have discouraged any man or woman had the cause been less worthy, or had the community been less wholehearted. Not once did the community allow the supply of any scarce items to fail. Sugar, meat, mayonnaise, coffee, drinking cups, candy and all the other items civilians scrambled for were made available unceasingly to the girls.

    Troy and Miami County presented a united front for a powerful and lasting humanitarian purpose. These girls were Troy's dedicated and unsung ambassadors to the many who stood in harm's way in defense of our freedom and liberties. The girls gave out thousands of baskets and shopping bags of food and hundreds of gallons of coffee, milk and lemonade. On behalf of a grateful region they expressed gratitude to the many troops including French, Chinese, Canadian, Scottish, Irish, and Australian troops. The entire 5th Armored Division of General Patton's Army, colored troops, WAVES, WACS and others were among the visitors hosted at the canteen.

    Troy and the region's reputation was enhanced immeasurably by the girls constant vigil. Sometimes a simple event is so powerful, so compelling, yet so routine that it can only be dealt with by leaving it to future generations for interpretation.

Acknowledgments

When Karen Purke mentioned there was a canteen in Troy, it took me by surprise. In years past I had spent many a lunch hour at the B & O station. I had briefly worked across the tracks at the former Gummed Products Company, yet this event had gone completely unnoticed. I had heard some church ladies met some trains with a food basket, but nothing more. In the biginning no one seemed to know anything about it.

While writing the story of the Lima Canteen, it was mentioned the two organiztions were coordinating their efforts from time to time, so it had to be more than what I knew about. Finally hitting on an article in the *Piqua Daily Call*, I found more articles and decided itwas time to go read the *Miami Union*. From there came a fascinating and untold stroy about Troy's canteen.

Patrick Kennedy and Barbara Besecker at the Troy Local History Library hauled out microfilms. Barbara and Judy Hemmert made phone calls and to my amazement volunteer names started coming, and there were many new stories. Suddenly the story had a great deal of meaning and it was far beyond anything I knew. To those three I am grateful.

Charles Bates of the Allen County Historical Society at Lima, Ohio, provided copies of railroad timetables for Troy along with access to other railroad materials.

Marlene Reid gave very sharp portrayals of her time as one of the canteen girls. Mary Margaret Gray added considerable insight. Doris Hislop shared very vivid accounts of her experiences. She was one of canteen girls at the station on Christmas Eve 1944 when a surprise Troop Train came in. Her recollections of the Troop Train coming in at the moment of the surrender of Japan in 1945 were extraordinary.

Betty Baldwin, daughter of Mary Tooley was the youngest canteen girl at the age of six. She shared her recollections and provided most of the known photos along with the loan of the original letters of appreciation written by the soldiers. I am indebted to her for the use of those materials.

Mary Lee Clawson offered exceptional recollections, as did Helen Hawkins.

Mary Lou Nordmark offered vivid descriptions of her times working there.

Patricia Furrow offered many comments about her experiences and of the Canteen picnic with the British soldiers.

Every conversation with a newly discovered canteen lady revealed new stories. Jackie Dierks, Rosemary Deaton and Lois Barnhart all offered unique stories and added details. Jackie helped to fill in the blanks about the mobile canteen trailer. Unfortunately, I was not able to locate any photos of it.

Keith Bader dug into the old photos files of Hobart Manufacturing seeking to discover whether any photos were still in existence. Unfortunately, none could be located. To him I am grateful.

Roland Davidson, a Troy soldier whose train stopped at the canteen made his heart-warming story known, William Roop, a 12-year-old paper boy during the war, shared his marvelous stories of meeting those trains and donating his newspapers to the soldiers.

Other people called to help locate the canteen girls. Isabelle Hawkins called to tell me two of her sister-in-laws had worked at the canteen.

To all of these people I am grateful.

Dedication

To:

The Junior Canteen Girls

and their mothers

Mary Tooley
Sarah Attenweiler
Ruth McWilliams
Loretta Pour
Ellen Abshire
Miriam Hartzell
Mary Hobbs
May Butler
Opal Scott

... and the other women and men
who gave their time
to see to the comfort of strangers.

The world is a better place because of them.

Contents

Chapter 1
    You Got Any Magazines?   11
Chapter 2
    Establishing the Canteen   17
Chapter 3
    Running the Canteen   38
Chapter 4
    The Community Rallies   58
Chapter 5
    A Christmas Never to be Forgotten   67
Chapter 6
    Those Last Months of War   80
Chapter 7
    The Troops are Coming Home   102
Chapter 8
    We Won't Let the Boys Down   114
Chapter 9
    The Flowers are From Tennessee   124

Roster of Identified Volunteers   130

Canteen Advisory Committee   131

Identified Organizations
    Supporting the Canteen   132

Gift Boxes Prepared by the Canteen for
    Veterans Hospitals   134

Bibliography   135

*"Do Unto Others
as ye would
have them
Do Unto You"*

The Golden Rule

From a sign that hung in the Junior Girls Canteen.

The West Street Ambassadors

A group of soldiers pose with the conductor of a B & O passenger train. They have just been served by the Junior Girls Canteen at Troy, Ohio during WWII. -- *Collection of Betty Baldwin*

Chapter 1

You Got Any Magazines?

WWII was in full swing and the American Military was mobilized as never before. Most of them were moving by rail and it was a daily routine to see troop trains passing through Troy, Ohio. *"Let's do something to help out the soldiers."* It was the thought of a group of Troy housewives, including Sarah Attenweiler, Ruth McWilliams, Mary Tooley, Loretta Pour, Ellen Abshire, Miriam Hartzell and Mary Hobbs. But what could they do?

Over at the Baltimore & Ohio Railroad station another troop train pulled in. Phyllis McWilliams, Mary Lee Mumford and other teenage friends were back over there again to see the troops and chat while the train paused for a water stop. Came an inquiring voice from the open window of the coach, *"Hay, you got any magazines us boys can read?"* The girls giggly response was, *"No, but we'll run home quick and see."*

They ran home to see what they might raid from their homes for the soldiers sitting in the train just a block away. They lived near the Baltimore & Ohio Railroad at Troy, Ohio. The passenger trains stopped for water in this Midwest community.

Girls have been going to see boys go off to war

on the trains since the Civil War days. This was a part of the American tradition.

Mrs. Ruth McWilliams and Mrs. Mary Tooley, went over to the tracks one day just to see what those teenage girls were up to. Too many magazines were disappearing from the stand at home and the girls always seemed to have a new tale of some soldiers on the train. Mary was astounded by what she saw, standing on the station platform looking, searching for some way to do something for the soldiers. Another train of the Baltimore & Ohio Railroad was pulling to a stop at Troy, Ohio. In the coaches were soldiers, soda jerks and farm boys, teachers and dentists, students and lawyers and service station attendants, iron workers and store clerks who in the prime of their lives went to war. Many had no idea where they would be going and it shown on their faces. She saw firsthand the real cost of war and it moved her in powerful ways.

The draft was reaching for the 18 year-olds. Many hadn't even completed high school. She saw many of the local fellows step onto the coaches in prior months as they headed for an induction center. She saw a few of Troy's own sons pass through on Troop Trains. The long days of war were wearing on this lady. Eighteen months of terrible war and over 3,000 local boys had gone, many from this very platform. Every day the newspaper was filled with stories of horrific battles in Italy, France, Germany and the Pacific. Every week the newspaper carried stories of local boys, neighbors who were missing in action, injured or worse. Some powerful force deep inside her heart drew her to do something. She had to give those boys in uniform something to comfort them and provide a few moments of distraction.

The ladies had read stories about Margaret Clingerman's New York Central Auxiliary canteen at nearby Bellefontaine, and Ellouise Larsen's AWVS canteen at Lima, 51 miles north. Troy was not a railroad town, not even close, but every passenger train did stop for water, usually about ten minutes. That was all the time she needed.

Ruth and Mary walked home, pondering what to do. It was just a short block across the park over to the Tooley family home on Union Street.

It started on a Summer day in August 1943. The look in those soldiers eyes had moved the ladies to provide food. They started baking cookies - lots of cookies! She and her friends gathered magazines and anything they thought might help. The next day Mary, Ruth and others walked back over to the sandstone station of the B & O, armed with baskets of wrapped cookies. They intended to meet one of the six daily passenger trains between Detroit and Cincinnati and give the soldiers a home made snack and something to read. In their very determined way, those ladies and their daughters began handing the soldiers their extraordinary gift of compassion and kindness. It was cookies, home made cookies, magazines, newspapers along with cheerful smiles and words of encouragement.

The next day they repeated the gesture, this time taking a couple of the other young girls in the neighborhood along to help carry baskets of cookies, magazines and anything else she thought the boys might like.

Mary Lee Mumford-Clawson recalled those early days, *"We started scouring the neighborhood for magazines, and then when we saw the demand, started asking for fruit, cookies and other treats to give the boys."*

Mary Tooley was the wife of an upholsterer at Troy Sunshade. They were typical working-class folks and there were few dollars available to support her altruistic venture, but she'd do what she could with anything she and her friends could scrape together.

The first passenger train of the morning usually arrived in Troy at 10:51 A.M. It was north bound Number 56.

The railroad's water standpipes were just north of East West Street and across from the station. The ladies, with their cookie and magazine laden baskets were on the station platform along with the neighborhood girls. They asked the conductor to either send the boys out, or he might have taken the baskets and walked down through the train offering free cookies and magazines to the soldiers. When the baskets came back, they were empty.

This was the routine for nearly a year. It was

word of mouth that brought donations of cookies, doughnuts and pies for the ladies and their daughters to pass out to the soldiers on trains pausing at Troy. They weren't formally organized, did not represent any kind of organizations, just doing what had to be done.

This 1949 photo shows significant locations for the Troy's canteen operations at the railroad. The B & O tracks move from left to right across the photo. The small building on the left is "The Target," a telegraph office where the girls would go to find out when the next troop train was coming, or to keep warm. The stone building on the right is the B & O passenger station. Note the large water stand pipe (white pipe with arm) in the foreground in front of the station. South bound trains stopped there for water. The locomotive in the background is on the P & T Branch. The wooden depot in the center distance is that of the New York Central Railroad. This photo looks west. - - E. M. Neff photo, *author's collection.*

The West Street Ambassadors

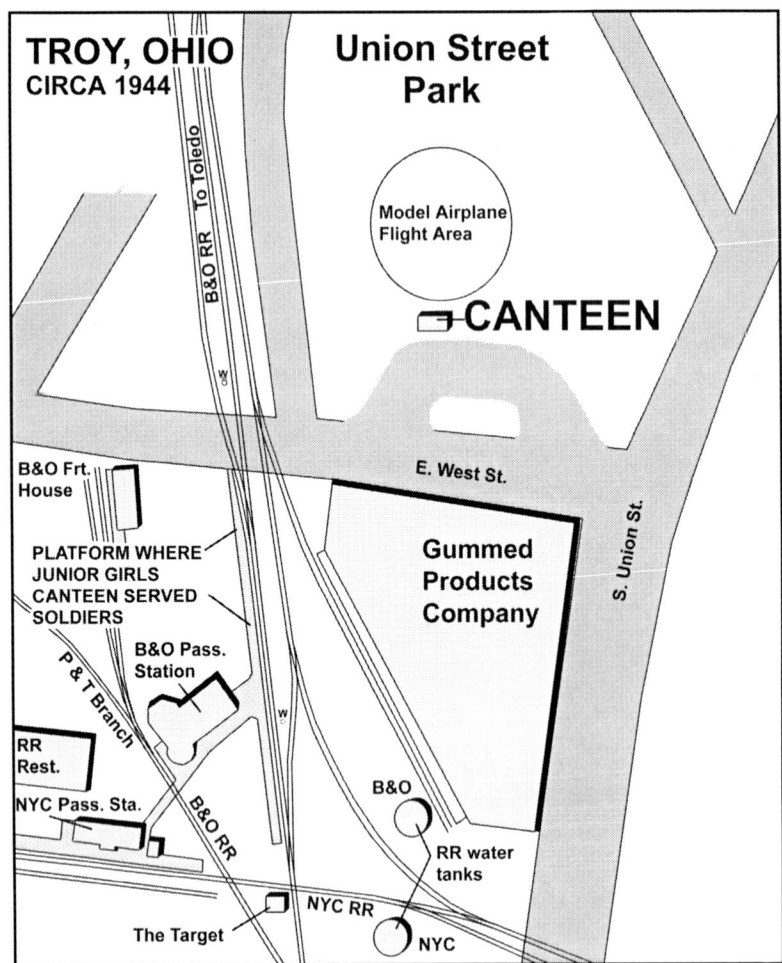

This map shows the location of the Junior Girls Canteen at Troy, Ohio during WWII. It was in Union Street Park, now known as Herrlinger Park. They served food on the platform of the Baltimore & Ohio Railroad station about 600 feet away. In early 1945, the girls received the donation of a trailer and parked it at the platform near West Street every day. The Tooley residence was across from the park on Union Street near the top right of the map. -- *Map drawn by Author*

Establishing the Canteen

Chapter 2

Establishing the Canteen

There were ten other community canteens operating along the railroads in Ohio, most in the western part of the state. All but three had been established in 1942. Six miles north at Piqua, they had a cookie group who met the trains on the days the newest recruits were leaving for boot camp. On north at Lima, was Ohio's largest canteen. It had been in operation for nearly nine months and with nearly 900 volunteers

Artwork from the Junior Girls Canteen flyer. While this illustration shows a girl wearing a skirt and sweater, many of the girls wore a red flannel shirt and blue jeans when they worked at the canteen.

they were feeding soldiers riding trains on three railroads.

When the Troy girls started meeting the trains, Germany had just been defeated in North Africa and the buildup to D-Day was well under way. Japan had suffered significant destruction to its naval fleet and the United States had established air bases in China from which they bombed mainland Japan.

Troops were moving through to a point of embarkation, some veterans and many wounded were passing through on the way to additional medical treatment. This canteen started without any fanfare or even any newspaper coverage. The adults forming the supervisors in the Junior Girls Canteen were, Mary Tooley, Ruth McWilliams, Sarah Attenweiler, Margaret Wilt, Ellen Abshire, Miriam Hartzell, Loretta Pour and May Butler. Initially there were 19 neighborhood girls, all between the ages of 6 and 16. Several of the girls were neighbors to the Tooleys, or daughters of friends.

According to Betty Tooley-Baldwin, the youngest of the volunteers: *"The ladies were all friends and homemakers. They were looking for some way to help the soldiers passing through on the trains."*

The ladies took the extraordinary step of organizing the Junior Girls Canteen to feed soldiers passing through town on B & O trains.

The idea was to help keep the soldiers' morale at it's highest. This Canteen project started in

Establishing the Canteen

the hearts of a few kind and compassionate people and grew to capture the imagination and support of hundreds in the region. The volunteer canteen workers' incredible spirit and selfless sacrifice was about to shine as never before.

They had no idea that before it was over they would feed hundreds of thousands of soldiers, new inductees headed for boot training, returning veterans, allied soldiers from foreign countries and wounded soldiers on hospital trains. They would become the town's and a region's ambassadors. These young girls and their mothers were witnesses to the tragedy of war on a scale never before imagined. Behind those pleasant voices, warm greetings and smiles were the best wishes and support of Troy and an entire region.

Within a few weeks of their expanding operation they quickly learned that the amount of food, the piles of magazines and drinks required could not be easily handled in their homes. A room or space was sought at the B & O passenger station, but there was none available. The organizers looked elsewhere for some place close to host their efforts. Mary Tooley looked across the street from her home and spied the small clubhouse at the Union Street Park (Herrlinger Park.) It had been used as a meeting room for a group of control-line model airplane enthusiasts. It had two rooms and a floor with walls, but no windows, no heat and no running water. It would do if the City of Troy would authorize its

The West Street Ambassadors

This September 1944, photo of the Canteen reveals a very young group of dedicated girls holding their original donation items of magazines and cookies. This picture was taken almost a year after the girls first started meeting the trains as a neighborhood project during the summer of 1943. These were the youngest girls to work at a trackside WWII canteen in the United States. The girls are as follows: left window, left to right, Alice Hobbs, Nancy Chronaberry and Rosemary Rudisill. In front of the door, Eileen Bergin, Betty Tooley and Eleanor Priest. In the door from left to right, Nanette Rudisill, Charlene Strome and Kathleen Kendall. In the right window, left to right, Phyllis McWilliams, Jeannine Kendall and Thelma Dohm. -- *Collection of Betty Baldwin*

Establishing the Canteen

Passenger Train Timetable 1943 - 1946
Trains initially served in bold type

Number	Direction	Arrival Time
58	NB	1:56 AM - No diner on train
57	SB	4:40 AM - No diner on train
56	**NB**	**10:51 AM - No diner on train.**
55	**SB**	**11:54 AM - No diner on train.**
54	**NB**	**2:50 PM - Carried diner**
53	**SB**	**7:24 AM - Carried diner**

Taken from the Baltimore & Ohio Railroad Timetable is the schedule for the daily passenger trains stopping at Troy during WWII. The Girls canteen decided to serve the four daytime trains, two of which did not carry a dining car. In early 1945, the girls announced they would serve all six passenger trains in addition to all other troop and hospital trains. This added another four to six trains daily. All of them stopped at Troy for locomotive water.

occupancy.

  They approached the City Fathers with their idea and were quickly granted its use. It lacked both lights and heat. The building was across the tracks, about 600 feet from the B & O station.

  In the meantime, the ladies were working out of their homes making food, but it was not an easy task. Mary Tooley lived closest, just across the park from the station, she took the lead in this project. Sarah McWilliams was right across the street and Mary Hobbs lived behind the McWilliams. Making food in home kitchens was the practice for about the first year the canteen operated.

By mid-1944, local businessmen were being solicited for donations of building materials and labor to fix up the newly acquired canteen facility. It was little more than a shack. Miriam Hartzell ask her husband to have counters built, and shelves installed. A hand meat grinder was quickly secured.

The Troy Elks Lodge gave them a telephone and donated service fees. The City of Troy provided electric, wired the hut and installed lights as well as adding lights throughout the park. The Parks Department also gave the park a general cleaning and installed playground equipment.

By the summer of 1944, the simple building housed Troy's Junior Girls Canteen. It was used as a modest food preparation kitchen and magazine storage. The girls and ladies had to pack baskets and bags with food, magazines and games, then walk from the park to the station just ahead of the arrival of each train and pass out the food to soldiers. It was a lot of work and took a strong commitment for the comfort of total strangers.

They learned that for each coach of soldiers they needed about three baskets of food. That would include sandwiches, desserts, snacks, and sundry items such as magazines, playing cards, post cards and so on. For each scheduled passenger train that carried perhaps eight coaches, would require 24 baskets of food. The Troop Trains often ran at 22 coaches requiring 66 bas-

Establishing the Canteen

A group of the Canteen girls in the Canteen building surround a picnic table stacked full of the items that will be packed into baskets and bags for the next train of soldiers. Included in the itmes are puzzles, checker boards, post cards, sandwiches, books, magazines, newsapapers and pies. This photo was taken March 6, 1945. The girls, from left to right standing are Jennine Kendall, Charlene Strome, Doris McMath, Nancy Chronaberry, Marlene Pour, Rosemary Rudisill, Mary Lou Scott, Eileen Bergin, Phyllis Shane, Patty Fox, Helen Turner and Marilyn Chase. Seated on the table in front of Marilyn Chase is Lois McWilliams. Seated to the left front of the table is the youngest volunteer, Betty Tooley. -- *Collection of Betty Baldwin*

kets. They were being carried across the tracks, or loaded into someone's car or put onto a small three-wheel cart or wagon. This was happening several times a day. Adding to that, it was not usually known when a Troop Train would be coming. Were it not for some discrete communications between the railroad and the Canteen, they would largely have been unprepared to greet the soldiers with adequate food.

The ladies realized the value of their work and the need for greater community involvement. They found it in Mary Tooley, who commenced writing some moving articles for the local newspapers. After the first stories appeared, the towns' people quickly stepped forward without hesitation in full support of this profound gesture of care. It was through the canteen worker's gestures toward the soldiers, that the good people of Troy, Piqua and Miami County began an incredibly powerful and determined gesture for the soldiers' benefit.

This project was not something orchestrated by the government or Red Cross. It was a group of friends and their daughters who took on this daunting task. All the food, all the services, all the hours of work were volunteered by private citizens and local businesses. This was the only canteen in the United States predominately staffed and operated by teenage girls.

With hearts of gold that truly shown through, on that Summer day in 1943, this oasis quietly began serving the traveling soldiers. The girls

Establishing the Canteen

were out of school for the last of summer and their mothers were homemakers so there was time to meet the trains every day and begin distributing the good cheer and comfort to those many soldiers on the trains. The girls weren't supposed to serve the trains from the station platform, but that rule was quickly relaxed when it was realized that street-crossing service was not sufficient to serve long trains.

The Canteen mothers quickly discovered their meager donations were not covering the needs of the canteen. They needed help with supplies, contacting friends, businessmen and civic leaders regarding their unique project. They were seeking support in any way possible to help those who were standing in harm's way. The response was immediate and positive. The root of American generosity and patriotism was awakened on a level never known before. Small gestures and kindness poured out that when multiplied, became Troy and a regions pride.

Miriam Hartzell's kitchen became a significant food preparation center for the canteen. When the family cook was not busy with the family needs, she was baking cupcakes, cookies, making another batch of cookies or mixing ingredients and making-up sandwiches for the next train. Mrs. Hartzell would go to the canteen two or three times a day and when troop trains or other special trains were coming in during the night.

By August 1944, the Canteen usually opened

around 10:00 AM and the girls were there until about 8:00 P.M. They planned to meet the four daytime passenger trains on the B & O plus any second section trains, Troop Trains and Hospital Trains. It was a herculean task that the ladies

This March 1945, photo shows several of the mothers in the compact kitchen area of the canteen building making sandwiches and packing baskets for the next train. The ladies in this photo from left to right are Miriam Hartzell, Sarah Attenweiler and above her is May Butler. The five people gathered around the table are, standing, Mary Hobbs, Ruth McWilliams and Ellen Abshire. Mascot Mickey Attenweiler is standing in the lower right and Mary Tooley is seated in front of the telephone. The ladies at the table are putting potato chips into individual wax paper bags.
-- *Collection of Betty Baldwin*

undertook, when they decided to cater to the nation's uniform military personnel passing through town.

At Troy, the Baltimore & Ohio passenger trains all took on locomotive water while at the station. It afforded about ten minutes for the canteen girls to make their offerings to the soldiers. When time permitted, the military travelers would get off, stretch their legs and get a bite to eat.

As the demands for rail passenger travel increased, more trains were put on and the demand for more food and more volunteers was met without hesitation.

There was no constant flow of passenger trains, but as war demands increased, the volume of troops on a single scheduled train would have to be scheduled as multiple trains, called Sections. In peak times a single scheduled train could be as many as two or three separate and closely following trains. There were breaks between arriving trains, sometimes three hours. These gaps were closed as one train of multiple sections would show up at the Canteen, usually with ten to twenty minute separations of time. The B & O operated two scheduled morning trains that called at the station between 11:00 A.M. and Noon. A train came in at about 3:00 P.M. and one early evening train at just about 7:30 P.M.

Trains Number 55 and 56 were all-coach trains that did not offer food service. That made the canteen very attractive to the soldiers. For those

Items Offered at the Canteen

Sandwiches
    Ham Salad
    Cheese Spread
    Peanut Butter

Cakes
Brownies
Doughnuts

Cookies
    Peanut butter
    Oatmeal
    Molasses
    Sugar
    Gingerbread

Pies
    Pecan
    Cherry
    Other pies

Hard boiled eggs

Candy bars
Other candy
    Hard Tack
    Sugar Creams
    Fruit Balls
    Chocolates

Beverages
    Coffee
    Milk
    Hot Chocolate
    Lemonade
    Coca Cola

Potato Chips
Cigarettes
Matches
Tobacco
Chewing gum
Ice Cream
Magazines
Books
Newspapers
Post cards
Writing paper
Pencils
Telephone calls
Telegraphs

Games
    Chess
    Checkers
    Dominos
    Puzzles
    Cross-word Puzzles
    Playing Cards

Fruit
    Apples
    Bananas
    Tangerines
    Oranges
    Peaches
    Pears

Establishing the Canteen

who happened to get a ticket on those two, their only option for food while in transit were the canteens at Lima and Troy. Number 53 and 54 the *Great Lakes Limited* carried dining cars, but food was expensive.

The ladies quickly learned a lot of the soldiers traveling on regular passenger trains were not being fed by the government and did not have a travel voucher to cover travel expenses.

The boys going home on furlough or traveling at their own expense were often downright hungry. The food in the dining car was expensive. Soldiers had traveled great distances without food for two or three days. A soldier's meager pay likely did not allow for the purchase of meals.

Once a week the latest draft notices filled the local papers. In mid-1944 the weekly departure of military inductees from Miami County was anywhere from 25 to 80. Many departed at the station and took Train Number 55 south to Cincinnati and the induction center across the Ohio River at Fort Thomas, Kentucky. Others made a connection at Dayton, heading for Fort Hayes in Columbus. The routine of sending the local fellows off to war had been going on nearly 30 months when the canteen project was started.

In those first few days of meeting the trains at the station, the ladies had to explain to the train conductor of each passing train that they were offering free food for the soldiers and begged for him to pass the word. The crews on Number 55 and 56 were happy with the new food resource.

Their trains offered no food service. The porters on Number 53 and 54 made every effort to see that the soldiers knew there were trackside canteens at Troy and Lima. Because the railroad had fewer trains, their conductors tended to come through every day and quickly made friends with the canteen girls. It helped and the soldiers knew what to expect on their journey through Troy.

That should have been enough to make every soldier rush off the train, but the ladies found it otherwise. A number of the USO and Red Cross Canteens charged for food, snacks and other items the soldiers obtained at these entities. According to Doris McMath-Hislop, one of the 15 year-old volunteers. *"The boys were wary of our canteen at first. They would look but hesitate to step up for food and drinks. When we told them it was all free then they'd come. It took us only a few minutes to learn how they were being treated at the Red Cross canteens. Many of those men were war hardened veterans and they didn't have much money."*

Many of the soldiers were teenagers and young men in their early twenties. This was their first time away from home. Some of them might never come back, others were coming through as casualties of war. They rolled into the station and were warmly greeted by the girls.

A soldier traveling to and from a furlough often made it known he saved his meager pay for months and even borrowed from other soldiers

Establishing the Canteen

In a downpour of rain south bound Number 53 is met and soldiers graciously served under a patio umbrella. This scene was played out many times between 1943 and 1946. The mothers manning the cart this night are Mary Hobbs, Ruth McWilliams, Mary Tooley and on the far right, May Butler. -- *Collection of Betty Baldwin*

in order to get passage. He was able to spend a few days at home with his family, but lacked money to buy food. Many of America's finest simply went without food for the days of personal travel. Troy's Junior Girls Canteen became a most welcome oasis. The trains would slow down and the weary look on their faces suddenly perked up as they spied the young girls, each carrying baskets and bags of food, magazines and other items. The soldiers on many trains were fed through the coach windows, the girls lifting the basket high so the men could reach in and take things.

Mary Lou Scott-Nordmark, reflecting back to the trains pending arrival, *"Mary Tooley would have us space ourselves along the platform so that each of us would be about even with one coach. Mary took the first coach herself, and when the train would stop, if the fellows weren't allowed off, we handed up the bags and baskets of goodies. If she needed to discipline one of us girls to get our attention, she'd space that girl down beyond the end of the train. We'd have to carry our bags further and if perhaps there weren't enough coaches, then we'd carry our bags back and wait for the next train."*

The fellows would ask the girls for their names but War Department regulations prohibited disclosure. The girls figured if they wrote their names and addresses on slips of paper and stuck them inside of magazines, that would likely get the job done. It had to be done on the sly as their mothers would certainly put an abrupt end to that practice.

Soldier's letters began to come, the girls wrote hundreds of letters. A few of the veterans and the Canteen girls were still corresponding forty years later. Some of the soldiers came to Troy after the war to meet and thank the girls in person.

Establishing the Canteen

Until early 1945, the ladies carried baskets and large paper shopping bags of food and magazines over to the platform. They put the bags on the Troop Trains and baskets onto the regularly scheduled passenger trains, the baskets would be returned the next day. As the days went by the soldiers started getting off of all trains. With the appearance of the mobile canteen trailer at the platform in 1945, the need to put food baskets on the train was lessened.

Soldiers could be seen straightening up their appearance as the train slowed. They started jumping off and making a dash for the trailer. Some took their food back to the train and ate it there. Others stood around on the platform and took in a little fresh air, the stillness of the solid ground and enjoyed the food.

Marlene Pour-Reid recalled, *"We had ham salad, cheese spread and peanut butter sandwiches. The filling was put between slices of bread and put into a wax paper bag. They were neatly stacked into the baskets and bags."* Doris McMath added, *"Our peanut butter sandwiches were a slice of bread with a thick smear of peanut butter, a leaf of lettuce and the other slice of bread was smeared with mayonnaise. We went through a lot of peanut butter!"*

During the winter the canteen was always cold. Mary Margaret Rush-Gray crisply recalled that they would be over there in the winter making up sandwiches and filling baskets and bags with their coats on.

The West Street Ambassadors

On every train there were Military Police. They were part of the Military Police Train Guards. In their white spats and white hat, they rode major routes and worked with railroad police. There were also members of the Navy Shore Patrol in the unit that rode all trains through Troy. The MPs and SPs that rode trains were stationed at Cincinnati. They checked the travel papers of all G.I.s and handled other tasks such as getting sick soldiers from the train to hospitals, making travel arrangements for stranded servicemen who found themselves without funds and in providing first aid. Theirs was an easy task at Troy. They simply announced the coming Canteen stop and got off the train to make sure the men weren't left behind.

Soon after the girls began the project, letters started arriving at the home of Mary Tooley, expressing the soldiers' appreciation. The letters became as important to the ladies and the community as the food they were providing. They were not only letters to the Canteen girls but to all of Troy and Miami County. The newspaper saw to the publication of a few every week. One such letter came in September 1944.

"I'm writing to thank you for your thoughtful kindness in giving us the magazines, cards and cookies. I was on a train that passed through Troy on September 7. I originally came from Connecticut and the thought of going so far from home was bearing heavy on my mind, but your little gifts cheered me up and made the trip

Establishing the Canteen

much more enjoyable."

The local newspapers, *Troy Daily News* and *Miami Union,* took an active interest in the daily activity, routinely reporting donations, needs, wants and importantly, the letters of thanks and gratitude.

It was all worth printing those letters. It was a rallying point in the community, a dividend for their personal investment in the efforts of the Canteen.

Sometimes the Canteen's importance to a soldier was other than a sandwich, pecan pie or a beverage. One day it was the powerful gesture of a phone call to an anxious family whose son had been held captive by the German Army.

Twenty-year-old William L. Reid, a Lima native-son, had been reported Missing-In-Action in Germany on December 21, 1944. He had been captured by the German forces. His status was only determined after his parents received a letter he had written while held in captivity in March 1945. When the American Army liberated the camp, just a week before the surrender of Germany, he was put on a troop ship and sent back to the United States.

Private Reid arrived at the Port of Charleston, South Carolina, and was promptly put on a hospital train and headed for the Veterans Hospital at Battle Creek, Michigan. On July 8, 1945, his train was routed via the B & O from Cincinnati, through Lima on the way north.

When he got to Troy that Sunday, he realized

he was on the very railroad that would take him through Lima, 51 miles north.

While the hospital train took on water, he asked one of the girls if they would call his parents and let them know he would be in Lima in about an hour. The request was given to one of the adult supervisors who hurried to the canteen and made the call.

The train left before they could let him know they were successful in putting a call through to his mother. It sped north for 51 very anxious and unknowing miles. At Lima his folks stood on the brick platform of the B & O station excitedly awaiting his arrival. As quickly as the train stopped he came off the hospital car. Wearing army issue pajamas and worn combat boots he was reunited into a most welcome embrace from his parents and to welcome tears of relief and joy. The visit was only ten precious minutes because he had to continue on and complete his medical examination at Battle Creek.

His mother wrote the following note to the "Canteen at Troy, Ohio," promptly upon returning to her home that very afternoon.

"Dear Friends:
I want to thank you for calling me this afternoon to tell me that my son, Bill, was coming through Lima on the B and O. We were at the station and had about ten minutes with him. These few minutes gave us the greatest possible joy for we feel assured

Establishing the Canteen

now that he is on the way to complete recovery.

"Please accept the enclosed money. It will repay you for your long distance call and also assist you with work in the future.

"I am
> Very Gratefully yours,
> Mrs. Leslie Reid"

Private Reid came back to Lima later that week to begin his survivors furlough.

The Canteen telephone was the vital link to help connect lonely soldiers with nearby relatives. Several times Troy fellows came in on Troop Trains and were able to run over to the canteen and call home. Others desired not to make contact with family. If no one was home, the ladies might try again later just to let the person know the soldier had tried to reach them and he perhaps wanted them to relay a message.

JR. GIRLS' CANTEEN
259 SOUTH UNION STREET
TROY, OHIO

This image is what the soldiers saw on the magazines and bags of goodies put on each train. This is the address where hundreds of letters of appreciation from soldiers were received. -- *Photo by Author, collection of Betty Baldwin*

Chapter 3

Running the Canteen

Junior Girls Canteen

The logistics of how the volunteers made this work were rather amazing. From modest beginnings ladies all over town and in the rural areas made baked goods; pies, cakes, cookies, and supplied the little park building without hesitation.

Canteen cookie bakes were held in homes throughout town, and perhaps 50 dozen cookies would be baked by a group of ladies. They also made homemade doughnuts and ladies would walk to the canteen with a basket filled to the top.

The grocers and bakeries usually provided 50 to 75 loaves of sliced bread every day. At peak times that number would rise to over 100 loaves daily.

Churches and several civic organizations opened their kitchens and volunteers showed up to make food. Mary Lee Mumford-Clawson cranked the canteen meat grinder many times. *"We made all of that ham salad with a hand-crank grinder. The eggs were all boiled in the homes of others. We ground all the ingredients and made it up just ahead of the trains."* Portions of the cheese spread and ham salad was made off-site. The Canteen shopping list included loaves of bread, meat, cheese, eggs, peanut butter, condiments, coffee, milk, flour, and sugar. The local grocers saw to many of the canteen needs. The day-old and two-day-old baked goods were routinely donated. Much of the bread was donated. Mr. Dewey of Dewey's Grocery generously donated many food items for which the dates were about to expire.

By October 1944, the town was supporting the project in a big way. The local dairies agreed to supply milk. The bakeries sold them fresh baked bread at cost, and often donated it. The butchers provided meat and ingredients for sandwich spread.

Farmers donated eggs. Orchards in the area supplied peaches, apples and pears at the sacrifice of those giving. Tropical fruits such as oranges, tangerines and bananas were purchased from local grocers.

The manager of the Blue Bird Bakery in Troy, Mr. Stevens, offered to donate pies. Some might have a broken crust, or a minor defect. His favorite was pecan, which became a speciality for the canteen. He saw to it the ladies had from 300 to 500 single serving pies every day, along with whole pies and other fruit pies, especially cherry. Pecan pies became the hallmark of the Junior Girls Canteen for all the soldiers. *"The single serving pies were all in cellophane bags, ready to serve."* According to Mary Lee Clawson. *"We got all the day-old pies and any that were perfectly good to eat but were not saleable such as a broken crust or slightly overbaked."* Over and above all the donated pies they purchased 12,000 additional pies monthly at $.75 per dozen.

The girls had another unique project, they made many of the checker boards and dyed the checkers at the canteen. Mary-Lou Scott helped with the making of the games. *"We dyed the little wooden disks red or black outside in a bucket and let them dry. Some of the girls would paint the blocks on the checkerboards inside the canteen. Then we counted out the correct number of checkers, put them in a bag and fastened it to the checker board. We'd put several checker boards into the bags going on each train."*

Much of the community was rallied by articles in the newspaper, all written by Mrs. Mary Tooley, who often came to aid in other civic projects by talking directly to others in the community and asking for their help. She quietly saw to the needs of the orphans and invited the teenage girls to come to the canteen once a week after school and help. At Christmas time she made it her responsibility to go to the orphanage on Christmas Eve and to invite those who might otherwise be forgotten to come to her home and enjoy Christmas with her family. Santa always saw to it they received gifts.

The local societies, fraternal organizations, and Sunday school classes took up the cause and

Running the Canteen

in addition to food, had special collections to assist in covering the operating costs. Several times a day someone dropped by with fresh baked cookies or an arm load of magazines. Some men brought cartons of cigarettes,

People would bring their ration stamp for sugar to the canteen so the ladies could use them for baking sugar. Mary Tooley had a list of ladies who would bake cookies with any available baking supplies. Others would buy a pound

> A desire is being expressed by the club girls that there be enough women volunteers to help uphold the name of Troy along this railroad route while the girls are in school. These girls have met the troop trains throughout the summer and delivered reading materials and cookies to boys who are very depressed at leaving home, many of them knowing they are slated for overseas service and will receive their orders when they return to camp. The girls, young as they are, realize that much can be done to build up the morale of the boys as they pass through the city. They are very anxious that this work which they started and is now showing rapid growth be continued and thousands of boys each week may feel this human touch.
>
> August 24, 1944

of coffee and bring it straight to the Canteen and donate it. Ladies in neighborhood groups would get together on a regular basis and bake dozens of cookies or make doughnuts. It was not unusual to get 50 dozen doughnuts or that many cookies every day.

Fresh farm eggs came in by the basket full. The ladies would take them home, hard boil them and bring them back to the Canteen. They were peeled for use in the sandwich spreads or put into the baskets for the soldiers to peel and eat.

Everything was donated and in turn it was given for free to the soldiers who came in on a train. It was a sincere gesture of compassion and care. It was a community-run hospitality center that provided food and drink to more than 300,000 service men and women during the balance of 1944. Large quantities of food were going through the Canteen, and nothing was lost or spoiled because it was all used immediately. A lot of people gave a little bit -- consistently, and that was the secret to its success.

Life for everyone at home during the war meant daily sacrifice. Few complained because they knew it was the men and women in uniform who were making the greater sacrifice. To many at home, it became a game to make due with less.

Since February 1942, gasoline was rationed. Butter, sugar, coffee and 200 food items were in the rationing program. The fathers of several of the girls walked to work every day in order to preserve gasoline for necessary trips.

Local Rationing Boards were set up and operating, and many items required a ration stamp to buy. The fact that you had a coupon did in no way guarantee that you could find some! Various substitutes for sugar were used when possible. Corn-based sweeteners were in demand. Farmers used honey from their hives. Some baked goods used sweet apples and applesauce. When butter got hard to find, they started using margarine.

Not all foods were rationed. Non-rationed items included; eggs, fresh fruits and vegetables, dried and dehydrated fruits, fish and shellfish of all varieties except that in sealed containers, bread and cereals, milk, grain products such as spaghetti, macaroni and noodles, poultry and game, jams, preserves and jellies, mayonnaise and salad dressing and perishable cheeses. Chickens were doing their part for the war effort with a surplus of eggs, which the canteen could readily use.

The thoughtfulness of the Troy residents shone through as home cupboards were regularly inventoried to see what rationed items could be foregone for the sake of the Canteen and the soldiers. A large number of households routinely made sacrifices in the name of those in harm's way.

When meat was rationed, many households turned to their Victory gardens, and to fishing and hunting of wild game in order to supple-

The three-wheel cart used to meet all regularly scheduled passenger trains from 1943 until early 1946. Baskets of food were placed on it and soldiers could help themsleves. The basket in front of the cart would be placed on the train and returned empty the next day. In 1945 a canteen trailer was added and the need for the cart was lessened, although its use continued.

ment the diet. Complete vegetarian meals were common and a favorite dish, macaroni and cheese emerged. Ladies formed clubs to discuss the challenges that confronted them at a household level and to find ways to address the need to keep ever growing food demands satisfied at the Canteen.

By the time this canteen was started, meat shortages were common. The Canteen ladies established a basic sandwich menu of ham salad, cheese spread and peanut butter.

The last week of September a train of new recruits came into town on their way to boot camp. The recruits were quite surprised to have been presented with cookies, pecan pies, magazines and playing cards. The regular train came in near 2:50 P.M. and at 4:30 P.M. that day an-

Running the Canteen

May Butler is preparing to hand up a basket of snacks and magazines onto Number 53, the south bound train. This basket has the canvas sleeve with identification that allowed the soldiers to take it with them. Only baskets were put onto regularly scheduled passenger trains because the railroad crews would watch them and see to their return. Bags were almost exclusively for troop trains since they would not be returned.

other Troop Train pulled in with a medical emergency on board. A local physician was summoned and while the train was at the station, 800 soldiers stepped off to relax. While talking to the canteen girls and other volunteers, it was learned that most of the men on this train were returning veterans who had served in the Army Air Corps. Most had been overseas from two to three years. They were headed for Camp Shelby Mississippi.

The meeting on the station grounds became the first "Welcome Home" and the girls were so happy to extend it and show their appreciation.

A number of visitors were at trackside to watch the trains that day. Many were thrilled at witnessing the homecoming soldiers. The canteen had a large supply of full-size pecan pies and hundreds of cookies to be able to meet this unexpected train. The Eagles Lodge had just donated a carton of used playing cards, which were quickly distributed to the soldiers.

When the ill soldier was of sufficient means to continue, the soldiers reboarded and the journey continued.

"The soldiers on all the trains were flirts," reflected Jackie Ovenshire-Dirks. *"The girls just drank it up as they handed up the bags and baskets."*

As time went on the railroad conductors became familiar with the canteen. They would make the canteen known to soldiers on the train and if the crowd getting off for snacks was large,

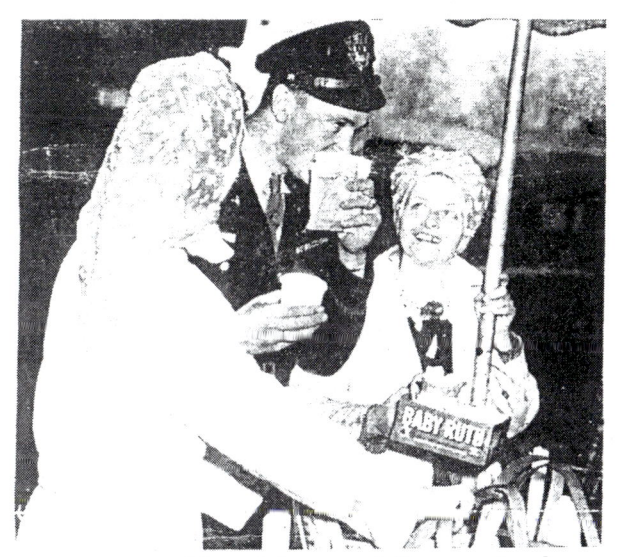

Two ladies stand beside a soldier as he is served on the B & O platform at Troy on a rainy evening in 1945.
-- From a canteen flyer

they might hold the train a few extra minutes.

Many times local residents came down to the station and witnessed these trains packed with young troops. They had to have felt a tug at their heart for these boys . . . and it was an incentive to go home and make a batch of cookies or to have felt glad for the things that were being done for them.

The Canteen effort had significant help from all the surrounding communities by August 1944. At Piqua, a longtime rival for the county court house, the Y.M.C.A. was setup as a drop-off station for food and magazines. Almost every week the *Piqua Daily Call* ran stories about the canteen encouraging Piquads to help in every way they could. Many gladly responded. The cub-reporter in charge of *Piqua Daily Call* articles was seventeen-year-old Rhoma VanDeMark, a high school senior.

A note from Zylpha Koehnle of the "Y" dated August 14, 1944, speaks of the Piqua effort. *"Well, it looks like we have made a start - we have already received quite a nice little pile of magazines - Readers Digests, National Geographics - Colliers etc. I hope they keep coming and am sure they will."*

Tipp City hosted several campaigns in solicitation for items. Every other Village in the County stepped up in support of the troops.

Donations came from individuals and towns in the surrounding six county region and from as far away as New York City and Chicago.

Sunday School classes, high school and grade school classes, ladies clubs, grange members, even groups of employees from local merchants and manufacturers stepped forward to help in any way they could.

By the end of October 1944, things had grown substantially. Monthly, about 30,000 soldiers were stopping and bills were near $1,000 for the unavoidable expenses such as rationed sugar, spoons, paper cups, and sandwich bags, shopping bags, wax paper and other food supplies.

Until November 1944, the people helping to support the canteen were loosely organized. As operating expenses grew, the need for a formal advisory committee came into being. That group

Running the Canteen

included Reverend A. M. Dixon, Coleman Scott, Herbert Ross, Treasurer, J. Camron Dungan, Mrs. Mary Tooley, Mrs. Noble Wilt and Mrs. Robert (Miriam) Hartzell.

The ladies could easily run the Canteen in two shifts during the day. During the summer months, when school was out, the girls would be there to cover the trains. When school resumed it required adults to be at trackside until the girls could get home from school. Each girl tried to be at the canteen a couple of days each week. Most came daily, and when called by Mrs. Tooley. "Its amazing how Mrs. Tooley, knew just when to call us," reflected Mary Lee lawson. "I'd get right over there and join the other girls making sandwiches at the Canteen. We made up sandwiches, then cut them in two diagonally and wrapped each in a piece of wax paper and put it in a basket or bag." A lot of times we'd be pushing the food cart across the track as the train would be whistling for the crossings at one end of town."

Passenger trains came and went, soldiers got off for just a few minutes and the ladies saw their faces, so many faces and just flecting glances. The girls of Troy offered brief encounters for homesick young Americans with the home cooked food and perhaps a smile or a kind word. It was a wonderful experience but went fast. One day a troop train pulled in and Helen Turner-Hawkins was passing out sacks of cookies. "*I walked up to the open door of a Troop*

The West Street Ambassadors

The Kid in Upper 4

"It is 3:42 a.m. on a troop train. Men wrapped in blankets are breathing heavily.

"Two in every lower berth. One in every upper.

"This is no ordinary trip. It may be their last in the U.S.A. till the end of the war. Tomorrow they will be on the high seas.

"One is wide awake...listening...staring into the blackness.

"It is the kid in Upper 4.

"Tonight, he knows, he is leaving behind a lot of little things - and big ones.

"The taste of hamburgers and pop...the feel of driving a roadster over a six-lane highway...a dog named Shucks, or Spot, or Barnacle Bill. The pretty girl who writes so often...that gray-haired man, so proud and awkward at the station...the mother who knits the socks he'll wear soon.

"Tonight he's thinking them over.

"There's a lump in his throat. And maybe - a tear fills his eye. It doesn't matter, Kid. Nobody will see...it's too dark.

"A couple thousand miles away, where he's going, they don't know him very well.

"But people all over the world are waiting, praying for him to come. And he will come, this kid in Upper 4.

"With new hope, peace, and freedom for a tired, bleeding world.

"Next time you are on the train, remember the kid in Upper 4.

"If you have to stand en route - it is so he may have a seat.

"If there is no berth for you, it is so that he may sleep. If you have to wait for a seat in the diner - it is so he...and thousands like him...may have a meal they won't forget in the days to come.

"For to treat him as our most honored guest is the least we can do to pay a mighty debt of gratitude."

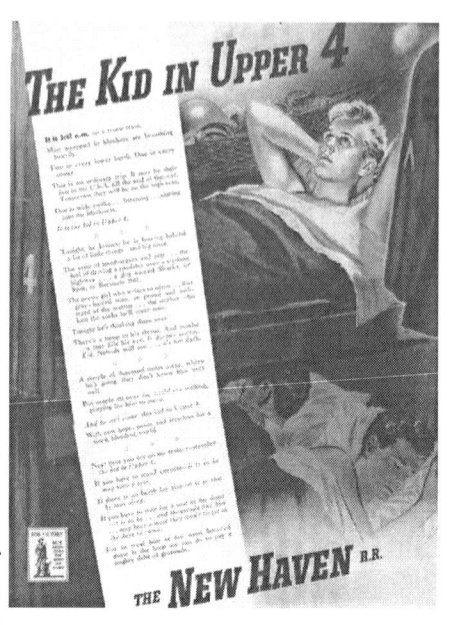

From a WWII ad by the New Haven Railroad

Kitchen Car and handed the cook a small sack of cookies. He extended his hand down to thank me. It was full of slime from the potatoes he had been peeling for the evening meal."

Every day soldiers, sailors, aviators and Marines traveling cross-country by train were given free coffee, sandwiches, dessert, cigarettes and magazines at the canteen before reboarding the train and moving on. Station-stops that averaged less than 10 minutes, yielded warm experiences, created cherished memories and lasting friendships.

A problem common to all of the canteens, many of the soldiers wanted to pay for the food. Their offers were humbly declined. Sometimes payment came as a letter with a donation enclosed, other times it was a letter from a parent, wife or sister with a donation.

Originally the Junior Girls Canteen consisted of 19 neighborhood girls, most from the east side of Troy. After the terrible cold snap of late 1944, their ranks quickly doubled.

Every day one or two ladies supervised about 20 girls, and other volunteers. It was generally split into two shifts, one for the trains around noon and the other covering the mid-afternoon train and the early evening train.

According to Doris McMath, *"I came in from school and changed clothes. Sometimes I did my homework first, then grabbed a snack and headed for the canteen. Other times I took my books with me and did my homework at the canteen between trains."*

Mary Lou Scott lived about three-quarters of a mile west. Her father was a railroad buff. He knew the locomotive sounds and the whistle calls, as well as the different locomotive types. He'd hear a south bound "special" or troop train about two miles north of Troy and say, *"Mary Lou, you'd better head over to the canteen."* She'd jump on her bike and peddle over, sometimes making it under the Race Street railroad bridge just ahead of the train. She'd peddle south of Crawford to the canteen, hurry into the canteen or up to the platform with the others and commence the ritual chore of passing up the bags and baskets of food and sundry items. She said, *"it was so exciting to see those troops and to serve them."*

If it was known that second sections were following or that Troop Trains were on the way, all the girls stayed there. Husbands and fathers might be called to help out.

The movement of all Military trains was a secret, but the ladies needed to know of coming trains in order to have enough help and sufficient food for the next flood of men. They learned to look at the color of the flags displayed on the front of the locomotive. If they were green, it meant another train was closely following. But there were other ways of finding the coming lineup of the trains. Just south of the station the Columbus-Indianapolis main line of the New York Central Railroad crossed the B & O. The signals and gates to control traffic over the crossing of the two railroads was handled from a small one-story telegraph office that the neighborhood dubbed "The Target." Another of the volunteers, Marilyn Chase, in her memoirs some years later wrote, *"Mrs. Tooley got acquainted with Mr. Cawley, who was dispatcher and worked in the tiny [building] by the tracks. He would never come out and tell us when but often 'accidentally' left the time sheet lay out where we could see it."*

Doris McMath remembered that when it was real cold several of the girls would walk down there to keep warm while awaiting the momentary arrival of a train. Often times when it was cold or dark, Mr. Cawley or Hutch, another of the telegraph operators would call Mrs. Tooley or one of the supervisors. She'd hang up the phone and tell the girls it was time to get busy making sandwiches and filling bags. At the appropriate time they would head for the station and soon enough a Troop Train appeared.

When the passenger or Troop Trains came in, those boys were off the train and on the platform in a flash. The girls had to make foods they could pick up and take with them quickly; sandwiches, cookies, pie, and drinks in paper cups.

Both McMath and Pour agreed, *"We fed every soldier on every train including the scheduled passenger trains, Troop Trains, Hospital Trains but we were told to steer clear of the P.O.W. trains."*

PLEASE LEAVE BASKET ON TRAIN RETURN TO JR. GIRLS CANTEEN TROY, OHIO

One of the canvas covered baskets put on the regularly scheduled passenger trains. Soldiers could help themselves to the items. The empty basket would be returned to the girls the next day. Other canteens in Ohio had coffee mugs that were returned and milk bottles that were also returned to their respective canteens after being emptied while in transit.

McMath added, *"We didn't even give the MPs on the P.O.W. trains any food. We were told to get back and we did."*

Mumford stated that in rainy weather the conductor allowed the girls aboard the train to pass out the food, magazines and games. *"We'd walk down the aisle of the coaches, which were narrow, and I'd be holding my basket longways in front of me offering food to the boys. During nice weather most times the soldiers got off the train for food. We weren't allowed to serve the hot coffee, that was left to the mothers who supervised."*

On Troop Trains where access was restricted or the soldiers weren't allowed off, the girls put three bags of food on per car. The baskets were put on scheduled passenger trains and usually came back on the next train or the next day with the conductor. The girls devised a unique method for getting the baskets back. They had a white canvas fabric sewn together to cover the outside of the basket. In large red letters were printed, "PLEASE LEAVE BASKET ON TRAIN, RETURN TO, JR. GIRLS CANTEEN, TROY, OHIO." Sometimes the baskets came back in a few hours on the next train, other times the baskets came back the next day, usually in the company of the Porter or Conductor.

Opposed to making up individual bag lunches as other canteens around Ohio were doing, they made up large shopping bags of food, snacks and sundry items. Recalling her time at the Canteen, Mary Margaret Rush-Gray observed, *"We made up the sandwiches, and placed them in wax paper bags or wrapped them, then put stacks of them into several shopping bags along with pecan pies and cookies. Another bag or two would be full of magazines, newspapers, cigarettes, matches and one bag would have playing cards, games, puzzles, writing paper and pencils. At first we carried all the bags over to the platform, but a little while later we got a three-wheel cart. Later we got a trailer pulled by an old Model T."*

Betty Tooley went on to say, *"The bags would be handed up to the Conductor on the Troop Trains. The Porter and a couple of soldiers might come down and get the bags from the ladies on some trains."*

At first all military personnel were restricted from getting off the Troop Trains, and all food was handed up, but later the rule was relaxed and the men were allowed off, especially the soldiers returning from battle.

All the volunteers agreed, *"We waved to every train as it departed. The soldiers who got off the many trains seemed so happy after they had gotten the food and snacks. Many times we heard many 'Thank You' expressions as the trains passed by. They would all be waving."*

Since this canteen did not open until a year after the war had been declared, the sorrows of battles were well known back home. Local soldiers had been injured, captured, were missing or worse. It made no difference to the volunteers, they were compelled by some higher purpose to be there for the boys on the trains.

The women were amazingly efficient. When a train came in they might not always know if it was going to have a large number of military personnel ready to step off for something to eat. When a large crowd got off the train, volunteers tried to keep enough sandwiches made up to meet the demand.

During the mornings of the school years the girls mothers and other volunteers staffed the

Running the Canteen

canteen. When the girls got there after school they were immediately put to work. Some made up sandwiches, filled bags and baskets with food while others sorted the magazines and bagged them in the magazine room. None of the girls really wanted to work in the magazine room, but none complained.

As word got out about the performance at the canteen, residents around town would come down to the station grounds as much to watch the canteen girls perform their duty as to see the soldiers.

The girls and women scheduled their time so that service would be available to all trains. There was always a group ready to meet the next train, regardless of the weather conditions. In the winter they dressed warmly: in wet weather they donned rain gear.

Troop Trains Served in 1944

January	13
February	16
March	27
April	27
May	38
June	25
July	38
August	49
September	31
October	18
November	31
December	15

This does not include regular scheduled passenger trains, hopsital trains or POW trains.
Source - Notes of Mary Tooley.

Chapter 4

The Community Rallies

What these wonderful girls and ladies did was to make the troops feel appreciated. They were heading for an infantry division or a battle field. Many didn't know where, or returning from duty, perhaps not in the best frame of mind, or wounded with a broken spirit and feeling alone. The selfless giving by the folks of Troy and Miami County was remarkable, but greater still was the giving they did out of their own deprivation. The resourcefulness they were driven to in order to continue the Canteen was awe inspiring.

The girls set donation jars around town and every week they would empty them, adding desperately needed funds to the treasury. Troy Sunshade set a jar at the guard house and every payday it would be full. Every Friday after school, the group of the girls emptied the jars. Reports indicate anywhere from $30 to $75 could be collected in single jar each week.

By early September 1944, a number of the manufacturers in Troy and Piqua as well as social lodges were taking an active interest in the Canteen. The list of one weeks donations included: Troy Elks - $50, American War Dads - $25, VanCleve School - $15, Christian Class 7 - $11, Hobart Brothers Company - $10, a sailor's father - $1, Lamda Chi Omega Sorority - $5, W. H.

The Community Rallies

Hobart - $100 of new pocket size detective stories, Hobart Brothers Company - 2,000 pencils, Charles Trostel - box of new pencils, Hobart Manufacturing - 1,000 post cards, Browers Stationers, 600 postcard views of Troy, National Biscuit Company - six large cartons of cookies

Mary Tooley and several of the girls are gathered around items for the next train. Left to right, standing, Charlene Strome, Doris McMath, Nancy Chronaberry, Mary Lou Scott, Rosemary Rudisill, Eileen Burgin, Mary Tooley, Phyllis McWilliams, Patty Fox, Helen Turner and Marilyn Chase. In front of Marilyn is Lois McWilliams, seated on the table, and seated on the left is Betty Tooley, turning to talk to Charlene. These are several of the young ladies who stood vigil along the B & O station platform between August 1943, and March 1946. -- *Collection of Betty Baldwin*

The West Street Ambassadors

This March 1945, photo shows British sailors on the platform getting drinks and sandwiches from Mary Lee Mumford and Phyllis McWilliams. Soldiers from at least six countries called at the canteen. British soldiers came to town for training and the Canteen provided them a picnic at the park.

and promise of all future sales at wholesale cost. Mayor J. D. Boak and employees of City Transfer Company, donation of transportation services to pickup magazines and supplies from the Y.M.C.A. at Piqua.

As the need became known to find more funds to keep the basic food supplies available at the canteen, several of Troy's civic leaders put their heads together to find funds. They hit on the idea of a charity fund raiser to be held at the Troy Country Club. It was hosted by the Ladies Social Committee of the Country Club. In early November, on the 10th, a Friday evening, the public came in great numbers. They were wel-

The Community Rallies

comed in by decorations of red, white and blue.

Mrs. Herbert Lange and Mrs. O. J. Neff drove to the canteen and picked up Mrs. Tooley and 21 girls. They were provided dinner at the Country Club then taken to the Mayflower Theater for entertainment, then returned to the Country Club where they were the guests of honor. There was a live band and many door prizes.

Mrs. Tooley was presented with several dozen red roses in appreciation for the ongoing work. She immediately shared her flowers with the girls.

Merchants all over Miami County sent merchandise as well as cash. Some of the items

This is the raffle ticket sold for the benefit of the Canteen at the fund raiser held at the Troy Country Club in November 1944. -- *Collection of Betty Baldwin*

included dressed poultry, coal, ice, furniture, books, war bonds, coats, canned food, fruits, and vegetables.

By the time the evening was over, $3,400 had been raised for use in feeding the soldiers. In addition, hundreds of people brought a huge quantity of magazines and playing cards for the canteen.

The event was acclaimed as the largest charity function ever held in Troy. Mrs. Tooley publicly thanked everyone.

Twelve year-old William Roop, was a newspaper boy in the neighborhood around the canteen. Every day he made it a point to meet the Troop Trians and give the soldiers free newspapers. Grateful soldiers threw him uniform patches and insignias. Once he even got a soft ball and bat from some returning veterans. Some days the soldiers got all his papers so he'd go back to the newspaper office for more. He did his patriotic best to support these many strangers.

As the long days of war moved on, people realized many of the soldiers moving through on furlough were making a long tiresome but necessary trip. Perhaps it was across a continent in order to see his wife, a new child and the folks once more.

A Troy soldier, Roland Davidson, was at Camp Breckenridge, Kentucky, when in September 1944, his wife gave birth to their first child, a son. Private Davidson had to get home if only for a few hours to see his son and make sure his wife

The Community Rallies

was Okay. With the help of another soldier from Tipp City, who had a car at the base, they got a pass and drove to Troy, where he had six hours with his new family. Their home was on South Walnut Street, just four blocks from the B & O station and the Canteen. They drove back to camp and made preparations for deployment to Europe.

In the early days of October, the Company boarded a Troop Train and in a few hours they were in Cincinnati where the train was switched to tracks of the Baltimore & Ohio Railroad and headed north toward Troy. There was no way to get his wife a message he would be in Troy for a few minutes so he would suffer a great anxiety and yet a spark of hope.

The train pulled into Troy and stopped for water. Private Davidson's coach was stopped dead across West Street and he could see Walnut Street three blocks west.

The canteen girls were all there, and so was the paper boy William Roop. None of the soldiers were allowed off the train so Roland opened the coach window and ask William if he knew where 909 S. Walnut was. In a flash the boy was running full speed for the Davidson home in hopes of summoning Mrs. Davidson to the train. As she was leaving the house she heard the train whistle as the train pulled out. The hoped for last minute encounter were dashed.

The soldiers with him were so glad for the treatment they received at Troy. He wrote the

Canteen expressing that he was so proud to tell the boys that it was his home town that treated them so royally and closed his letter with a plea: "Please keep up the good work."

Private Davidson's outfit was headed for the Battle of the Bulge. He was wounded by machine gun fire on Christmas Eve. He spent time in several hospitals in Europe and the United States before finally returning to Troy and his family.

The volunteers' encounter with these faces was brief. In Troy they were greeted with smiles and delicious food, the now famous Blue Bird pecan pie and the gestures to give them a small taste of home. For the Canteen volunteers it was an unspoken reality that some would not return. It was described as the unspoken heartache. They had to believe they would all come home. Everyone was aware of that reality when they picked up the newspaper and read stories of the kindness at the station. Readers also saw the story of the latest Miami County man killed in action or reported missing, followed by the names of the next seventy or eighty men from the area being inducted into the service.

Another Troy soldier, also with a wife and new born baby went absent without official leave just to see them once before embarkation to the Bulge. Sadly, he was killed there. His cousin, ten year-old Patty Kirkland, was determined to help others on the trains, and over her mother's mild objections, she rode her bike to the canteen and helped. She'd listen for the train whistle, grab her bike and go like the wind.

The soldiers who came in on those trains never forgot the warm greetings and hospitality on the B & O station platform at West Street. Even on the battlefield some of them paused to write a note of appreciation. Others thought of the kindness while being held in captivity by an enemy, it was their only way of recognizing the goodness shown by the people back in Troy, Ohio.

During the short years the canteen was in operation, many letters were received by volunteers from soldiers or their families who expressed thanks for the hospitality shown them.

The sister of one soldier wrote to the ladies of the Canteen in December 1944, having read her brother's story of how well they had been treated at Troy.

"*We at home were so glad to hear that there are such places as Troy, although we have never heard of any other boys from our town being treated as nice as my brother and his group were when they went through Troy.*"

Her brother had written about Troy from a base in England. While the Americans were on foreign soil, soldiers from many Allied nations were in the United States. Coming into Troy were soldiers from Canada, Australia, England, China and free French. All were welcomed to Troy by those young ambassadors at the station.

The enduring purpose of the canteen was to feed the soldiers and bring them some taste of home. One article stated, *"Much merriment is displayed by the traveling soldiers in the coaches after they receive their allotments of candies, cookies, apples, and sometimes even bananas, together with magazines, playing cards, and games that are put on the trains."*

A Major on a Troop Train, expressed to the girls before their train pulled out that their canteen was one of the greatest morale building organizations he had ever run across. He noted he had traveled the length and breadth of the United States. The boys on the train sent back the top of the pie box inscribed with the signatures of every officer on that train.

As the holiday season approached, every week there were notes in the newspaper thanking all the ladies around the area for cookies and asking for many more.

As more trains rolled into town, sometimes they found many of the troops had already retired for the night and were not able to offer immediate expressions of appreciation. The ladies put the bags of goodies on the trains anyway. One soldier who awoke the next morning to find bags and bags of food, pies snacks and sundry items wrote to the girls.

"Your bags that were set on the train were very much appreciated. This train was serviced at night as the boys slept. The books and games were just what we needed and we all felt the next morning like children getting up on Christmas, and it may be the only Christmas we have all year."

Chapter 5

A Christmas Never to be Forgotten

A terrible cold snap hit the Midwest just after Thanksgiving 1944, and lingered for several weeks.

As the Christmas season drew near, radios were playing new songs like "I'll be Home for Christmas," and "I'm Dreaming of a White Christmas." Mary Tooley began a campaign to make the community aware of the need to remember the soldiers who would be on the trains. She was determined to see that every soldier on trains during Christmas was personally given a gift by the fine people of Troy and the region. Suggested gift ideas included, match folders, razor blades, chewing gum, stationery, candy bars, handkerchiefs, Christmas cards, post cards, and pencils. She made an effort to mention, *"that anything you think your son might like would be acceptable."* Such thoughtfulness by strangers was sure to make the soldiers happy.

There was also a solicitation for homemade Christmas cookies. Mrs. Tooley stated, *". . . if there are some mothers who cannot bake cookies but wish to contribute this item, they should send their sugar stamps to the canteen and other mothers of soldiers will be glad to do the baking."*

The holiday season around the Canteen was a uniquely special time for the military visitors.

The West Street Ambassadors

Canteen volunteers witnessed those special moments, many touching. As the soldiers were being served, small groups of service men and service women would break into songs of Christmas carols. It was an impromptu gift to all of Troy. Soldiers in one car broke into A Capella chorus. It was picked up by more soldiers in adjoining cars. Singers were being spontaneously joined by others and soon the air was filled with gleeful harmonies from an entire train of appreciative soldiers. The singing soldiers were still harmonizing as the locomotive sounded its two whistle blasts and departed town. A few remember the unique warmth and that giving atmosphere. Their voices faded into stillness and calm filled the air after each coach had passed by and the train slipped away. It is possible that many volunteers who stood there in the power of that moment smiling, waved with tears of joy streaming freely down their cheeks. Never could a chorus have sounded so sweet or been so emotionally moving as what they witnessed in that moment.

By this time the girls had become known to the railroad crews. There was a colored porter on *The Great Lakes Limited* whom the girls came to know as Ralph. When he was on north bound Number 54, he'd get down, taking the baskets and bags from the girls so they would not have to be burdened.

One day just before Christmas 1944, he heard some of the girls wanted to go Christmas shop-

A Christmas Never to be Forgotten

ping at Piqua. He asked them to let him know when they wanted to go and he'd see about getting them transportation on the train. They did so, and on the appointed day, when the train stopped, they and their bags of goodies got on. This time they walked through the train passing out food during the six-mile trip north. They walked the aisles of the coaches until they reached Piqua, where Ralph took over their duties. He told them to be back at the station for the seven o'clock arrival of south bound Number 53. His routine was to manage the diner as far north as Deshler, then to take the south bound train back to Cincinnati.

When the train arrived at Piqua that evening, the girls boarded and were given their empty baskets. Both the baskets and girls were returned to Troy. The railroad never charged them for their passage that day. The train crew would not hear of charging them train fare after all they had done for the soldiers.

A most horrific winter started with a snow and ice storm on December 12. It took down power lines and made travel difficult. The four daylight trains were delayed by several hours. As holiday traffic peaked, trains continued on a one to three hour delay through Christmas. The temperatures continued to drop, hovering near zero for several weeks. The Canteen girls never missed a train. One B & O train came in and there were so many cars the ladies had to walk along the tracks, carrying baskets through snow, rain and mud in order to give good service.

The ladies and girls made sure the soldiers who would be coming through on Christmas were not forgotten. The week before Christmas many people spent their time at the canteen getting ready for the trains, not knowing the role they would play on a very cold and solemn Christmas Eve. They wrapped small gifts, made candy, cookies, cakes and did it with the esteemed satisfaction of giving in the service of others.

The citizens of Troy donated $145 for gifts, lots of candy, cigarettes and the famous Blue Bird pecan pies.

Just days before Christmas a train came in late one evening. Private David Lear from Tunnel Hill, 160 miles east of Troy, was on board. He had written his folks a letter but there was no place to mail it. Louis Tooley was at track side helping the girls, so he took it and promised the young soldier he would see that it was mailed. A heartfelt letter from his mother came to the Tooley home four days after Christmas.

"Dear Friend:

"We rec'd your letter and our letter from our boy which you also mailed. You have no idea how glad we are for this. He said in his letter he would take a chance on us getting it as he had wrote it in bed on the train. You sure are doing good work with your 'Canteen.' I know every one of them boys appreciate it. As so near Xmas, I

had mailed our boy Xmas boxes but am afraid he was moved out before he got them. He had been in Texas for almost 2 years, was home in November. We live 12 miles east of Coshocton, our boy said he went through Coshocton and sure hurt to know he was so near home yet so far. Again I say thank you for your Xmas party for those boys.

"There isn't very many families that don't feel the heart-ache of this war. And those that don't, really don't know much about it.

"Am closing and again thanking your husband in his risk of taking and seeing that we got our boys (Dave's) letter.

"Yours,

Mrs. J. C. Lear"

On a bitterly cold Christmas Eve, Number 53, the south bound train made its scheduled 7:23 P.M. stop. Many Troy residents were headed to their respective churches for services as the whistle of yet another train filled with soldiers brought a momentary reality to a desperate world situation.

The soldiers on that train were greeted with cheery smiles, best wishes for the season and given food and gifts. There were no green flags on this engine, meaning there would be no following section. The girls were chilled to the bone and quickly moved back over to the canteen to warm up. Perhaps they enjoyed a cup of hot chocolate and a cookie before heading home and to church for Christmas Eve services.

About that time the phone rang and Mrs. Tooley answered. It was Hutch over at the Target. He had bad news, sorta.... The dispatcher at Dayton had just coded a north bound extra for 9:00 P.M. arrival in Troy and it was a Troop Train with 14 coaches and 400 soldiers. Going to church was out, the warmth of home and family and the wrapping of presents and Christmas dinner preparations would have to wait. Suddenly there were 42 bags of food to be gotten ready, plus a whole lot more.

They barely had time to get more sandwiches made up and bags of food and gifts ready. Mrs. Tooley called all the help she could. In less than an hour they would surprise many soldiers from the 661st Tank Destroyer Battalion and show them the real spirit of Troy, Ohio. Santa was bringing the boys to them!

On that icy cold indigo night a very dedicated group of girls and ladies loaded everything into a few cars and drove it over to the station platform. In the solemn silence as stars filled a perfect night, from the south came the steady sound of a mournful whistle. The golden rays of the headlight illuminated the snow blanketing the tracks

The conductors who knew about the canteen were confident the Canteen girls would not let them down on this Christmas Eve. The soldiers were ready to hit the hay before they reached

A Christmas Never to be Forgotten

Dayton. It took quite a lot of persuasion to get them to stay up until they reached Troy. Two coaches of soldiers had retired before they reached "the best little town on earth." The men had been on this train since leaving Texas on December 22, they were destined for New York and embarkation to France.

Many of the girls, including a very cold, but dedicated 15-year-old Doris McMath, stood ready to play Santa as never before. She recalled the bitter cold. *"I had on boots, shoes, heavy knee socks, slacks, a snow suit, mittens and I was about frozen. We put many bags of goodies on that train."*

The Canteen girls, in the name of Santa Claus put on the train an amazing inventory of foods and gifts: Christmas cookies - bushels of them, pecan pies, Christmas candies - old fashioned hard tack, sugar creams, fruit balls and chocolate candies - playing cards, razor and razor blades, pocket combs, tooth brushes, stationery, postal cards, pencils, shaving cream, shaving soap, styptic pencils, tooth powder, books of the month, pocket size books, checkers, chess, dominos, puzzles, cross word puzzles, over two bushels of candy bars, each one wrapped in Christmas paper, in addition to cigarettes, matches, apples, oranges, tangerines, and magazines.

It is reported that 300 dozen cookies were at the canteen when word of the train arrived. On the train were four Troy boys. Two made themselves known, two other said they would rather not tell their names. Private calls were made on behalf of the boys to let families know of their brief stop and to perhaps make their Christmas a bit more joyful.

As the many bushel baskets and bags were loaded onto the train the girls heard remarks. "Who said we were the forgotten men in the world tonight:" "Let no one tell me there isn't a Santa Claus, I know better now:" and throughout the train as the girls and ladies walked along they heard expression of appreciation.

During that brief ten minute stop the lives of many soldiers were changed, as were the lives of the Canteen volunteers. Tears of joy were shed as a mournful whistle announced the continuation of a long journey into a silent night. By the time the girls were back at the canteen, church was over and maybe they sang a few carols on the walk back home.

A few months later a letter came from one of the men who was on the train that night. The letter is reproduced below:

March 5, 1945
Somewhere in Germany

My Dear Young Ladies:

Late last Christmas Eve, a troop train rumbled across the U.S. enroute from Texas to a P.O.E. The men were in their bunks but most of them were awake thinking of their loved ones

A Christmas Never to be Forgotten

and the Christmas Eves of years gone by. Being away that far from home on this particular night was pretty rough and the men's spirits were naturally very low. On top of it all, they had been traveling across the nation that whole day and no one had so much as wished them a 'Merry Christmas.'

Then an event happened that none of the men will ever forget. The train rolled into a town and baskets of neatly wrapped gifts were brought on board. The shout of "Merry Christmas" was heard in the still night. This event made all the men feel pretty good. They knew then that someone appreciated what they were doing.

You girls caused those men to fall asleep happy. For this we thank you with all our hearts. That welcome you gave us was a grand thing. Your gifts carried sentiment that was worth more than all the money in the world. Thanks again and may God bless all of you.

Gratefully yours,
Edward J. Krenek
Co. B 661 T. D. Bn. (Tank Destroyer Battalion)
c/o PM, New York, N.Y.

Three other letters were received from fellows on the train that magical night. One came from Jim O'Brien of Toledo, Ohio. He wrote it on February 2, 1945, from France, and started his letter with "To the Helen's of Troy." He hoped one day to come back and thank the girls in person individually.

Private John O'Connell wrote his letter of appreciation from France. Corporal Arthur Ciesielski wrote his note while moving across the ocean, December 29, 1944.

"Dear Girls:

"I am writing you a few lines of thanks for meeting us on that trip through Troy, O. We were all kind of down in the, shall we say dumps, until we heard you girls would meet us at the next stop. It wasn't much of a Xmas for us boys on the train until you girls came out that night. So thanks a lot for all you have done for us. The whole Company appreciated it, and thanks again for all you have done for us.

"Yours Truly,

Cpl. Arthur D. Ciesielski"

On Christmas morning the Canteen girls were back at the canteen in time to meet north bound Number 56 for its 10:51 A.M. arrival.

It was a repeat performance of Christmas Eve, including the cold weather. The girls all gave up a warm home and the atmosphere of Christmas morning to be there for those who had no such comfort as they moved toward the east coast and embarkation to Germany. For this

A Christmas Never to be Forgotten

they were warmly remembered in a letter signed by fourteen of the soldiers whom they served.

"Dear Girls:

"I will take this time to thank each and every one of you for the gifts we received on Xmas day. Most of the boys have travelled over the world and I think that is the first time that we have received anything like that. We are somewhere on the east coast and the weather is cold. How is it there?

"This Xmas was the first one that most of the fellows was away from home and maybe felt kind of blue. I know I did but you see we have to take things as they come. We hope that every one of the boys will be home by next Xmas. Well there isn't much more I can say so I will close by wishing each and every one of you girls the best of luck and a Happy New Year and the best of success through the years to come.

"Just Soldier Friends"

The next week a north bound train came in carrying four carloads of military. One car was filled with nurses and three cars with soldiers. The train was absolutely packed. Occupying two seats were five cadet nurses, trim and neat in their cadet blue uniforms, laughing and joking over the superfluous of humanity surrounding them. Three were precariously seated on the arms of the seats with their bags in the aisle. One recalled the fact that her grandmother had once lived in Troy.

One finally pulled a Dayton newspaper out and divided it into sections, giving a part to each nurse. Soon the train slowed to a halt. With the train stopped the nurses exchanged seats with each other, the ones formerly seated upon the chairs now settling into the cushion with a sigh of relief.

Several soldiers got off the train into the bitter cold, and just before the train departed, one emerged from the crowd of canteen girls with a basket containing cigarettes, magazines and fruit, neatly arranged for easy access. Close behind him was a porter carrying three more similar baskets and asking in a loud tone of voice for another service man to assist him.

Stopping at the seat of the five nurses, the youthful soldier, but a teenager blushed slightly and offered some contents of the baskets. He stated, *"Compliments of the Troy Junior Girls Canteen. They handed them to me for distribution."*

The nurses smiled as each accepted a magazine, a small sack of cookies, candy and an orange.

The porter and soldier took the baskets further along through the car giving each soldier playing cards, magazines, cookies and sandwiches. The scene had been repeated thousands of times.

A Christmas Never to be Forgotten

Happy smiles, cheerful faces, each soldier with a lilt to his eyebrows and a grin revealing his gratitude and happiness was the result of those gestures of kindness. The soldiers, were finding they were not forgotten, that they were remembered even in this modest way, it made their long boring trip more comfortable.

It was the many donations of food, gifts and cash from Troy and the region that made this service so important. It was all carried out by a group of teenage girls, handing up bags and baskets of food and magazines. Sometimes it was walking along the train, extending gifts and snacks through open coach windows, their shining eyes and girlish smiles making soldiers feel valued and their job much more important.

The girls were on the station platform when a sudden and prolonged cold snap put heating fuels at a premium. Coal and fuel oil shortages were hitting and everyone was asked to close their businesses one day a week in order to conserve. The Girls Canteen and its volunteers struggled on, not complaining as the many trains came through and the thousands of soldiers braved the cold for a sandwich and drink at the B & O platform.

Chapter 6

Those Last Months of War

    As the entire region began to realize the importance of the work the girls were doing, most outlying communities made an effort to support the canteen. Suddenly it was no longer just a Troy-Piqua-Tipp City project. Donations were coming from Shelby, Darke, Montgomery, Clark and Champaign counties.

    Mrs. Bernard Miller from Piqua, heard about the canteen and began making cup cakes and cookies every week, dropping her basket of desserts off at the Piqua Y.M.C.A. on the days when the truck would be picking up magazines.

    When ask why she was doing this she said, *"I do like to cook and I know how my nephew likes things from my kitchen. Just thought maybe some other boys away from home would too."*

    Everyone was suddenly getting into the act. Waste fats were being collected by the Home Council and the red points granted for ration stamps were donated to the Junior Girls Canteen for use in obtaining sugar and coffee.

    The Fletcher Community Grange held a family supper and ask each person to bring magazines for the girls. School children all around the county took up collections of magazines and change in support of the efforts of the canteen.

    The girls had become this region's ambassadors of good will. When they weren't able to be at the canteen, would listen for the distant whistle of the approaching train. They made it their business to make a dash for the canteen from wherever they might be at that moment. Into the canteen they would come, gathering up dozens of bags and baskets filled with cellophane bags of cookies, pecan pies, apples, oranges, sandwiches and magazines, heading across West Street to the station platform in time to meet the next train of soldiers. The gestures of kindness were deposited on the train. The girls waited until every soldier who was hoping that something different would happen, realized his wish.

For this work the girls only compensation was the thrill they received in the great receptions from the boys on the trains.

It was brought home in the simple words of a letter of appreciation penned somewhere in Europe in January 1945, by Tec 5 Richard W. Bowers.

"*Good Morning:*

In the not to distant past a troop train passed through your small but swell town. I am not at liberty to say when or where we came or to where we went. I believe that our intentions are apparently obvious. I do not doubt that most of us will never see that town again but then we still owe you an obligation that can be only partially paid for in words. The intentions can never be rewarded although I know that the physical ef-

fort was fully compensated for by the smiles and the thank you's of each and every one of us.

"*To us you are a symbol of all the other girls and women who will be waiting for all the boys that do come back. We know that when you give a soldier food, cigarettes and magazines you do it because you feel you are each helping out that certain fellow you are waiting for. Unfortunately he cannot thank you so that leaves the job up to the rest of us who may be able to find a little time to do so.*

"*Do not forget that we like above anything else to hear from you, and you, and you. Write often as you can and as much as you can and we will do our best to keep up our end despite other pressing business.*

"*Sincerely Dick Bowers*"

In mid-March 1945, a long Troop Train stopped in front of the Troy station. It was described as strung way up and down the tracks. It was hardly daylight, yet every window in every coach was packed with faces... faces of these kids who were on their way to "destination unknown."

Many of those young men should have been in high school, yet they were on their way to lands and events of global significance.

The Junior Girls Canteen met that train. Over thirty women and girls rolled out of bed early that morning. Instead of enjoying breakfast before leaving for school, they were at the canteen early to make up bags of food for the soldiers. They met it at the platform with smiles, waves, words of encouragement, and bags... bags filled to overflowing with magazines, playing cards, puzzles, games, candies, cookies, apples, pecan pies, postcards, pencils, stationery—and even a few cigarettes. How grateful the boys were for those gifts! The monotony of the trip was broken, and for a few moments at least, these young soldiers had a little touch of hometown kindness.

After the locomotive water was replenished, two blasts of the whistle were sounded and the locomotive set the train in motion. The girls and ladies stood on the platform and waved, hearing the expressions of thanks from total strangers. After it had cleared the platform, the girls headed for school. They would be back later in the day to service more troops, perhaps a hospital train. It might have passed through one or more of these girls minds that the boys in uniform might have asked them to go out for a movie and a soda if times were different. On this day these young men were heading off to defend them from a horrific evil that threatened the world.

Every day military personnel passed through Troy on the trains... soldiers, sailors, marines, Wacs, Waves... 1,000 a day-on average! Regardless of the hour or the weather, the folks of the Canteen met—not just some—but every train!

Hundreds of bags of food and sundries were

A group of ladies work in the Canteen, repackaging cigarettes and matches. They usually put three or four cigarettes into small envelopes for inclusion into each bag or basket. Left to right are Ellen Abshire, May Butler, Mary Hobbs, Ruth McWilliams and Sarah Attenweiler. -- *Collection of Betty Baldwin*

made up at the Canteen and put on those trains every week.

The girls had doubled their efforts and many boxes of cookies and other items were being sent to a number of service hospitals in nearby areas for the benefit of the wounded who were returning from overseas. They contained cookies, pecan pies, magazines, cards, games, in fact anything that helped to while away a weary hour or two. Boxes went to all three major Ohio military hospitals plus others in Virginia, West Virginia, Michigan, Indiana, Kentucky and Arizona.

By the end of January 1945, expenses were running over $800 per month for supplies. Mary Tooley reported that it cost about $.03 per soldiers for supplies and food. On March 1, 1945, there was $541.01 left in the treasury. The canteen board decided a public fund drive was necessary to meet the growing demand.

The sudden surge in soldiers prompted an urgent fund drive. James Mischler headed the campaign. When he realized just how short of funds the Canteen was, he made a personal call upon Vivian Fulker of the Troy Foundation, seeking an emergency grant of $500. It was followed up with a letter. In Mr. Mishler's words; *"It is very difficult to measure the good that is being done by the Canteen, just as it is difficult to balance up the investment of time, effort and money to other charitable projects. There are hundreds of letters available from service men and women that have poured in to the Canteen from literally everywhere, and they all sing the high praises of the magnificent service being rendered by the Canteen. I have personally gone through several big stacks of these letters quite recently for the purpose of culling them over for publicity ideas to be used in the coming drive. The spirit of genuine gratitude in them is quite marked. Many carry the thought of low spirits before arrival in Troy and happy singing upon departure. One boy wrote from the fighting zone in Europe that he and his outfit had talked about the reception in Troy many times. In fact, to his gang, Troy had become a sort of symbol typifying the warmth of home and what they believed was the real heart of the good old U.S.A. You can't weigh things like that . . . and such messages pour in from day to day. In fact, to be around the Canteen is to get caught up in a sort of infectious spirit that soon has one believing that perhaps this project is one of the tops of those in this community.*

"It would seem permissible now to tell you that last year over 350,000 service men and women passed through Troy, or about 1,000 per day average. Every train was met that had a person in uniform on it, and regardless of the time or weather. There is no doubt that these people of the Canteen have great sincerity, and their regard and compassion for the boys in uniform is simply tremendous.

"In addition to the work at the trains, the Canteen supplies a great number of parcels for various service hospitals. This activity is really quite large and a very important one, and which is not generally known.

"After carefully surveying the operations of the Canteen since its inception . . . and after observing the remarkable results that seem to have been obtained, it is the opinion of the Board that this is a most worthwhile project and one which by all means must be preserved and continued."

Those Last Months of War

A copy of the March 27, 1945, newspaper page soliciting funds for the Junior Girls Canteen. The ad was paid for by Troy's major industries. It was a powerful tool and the Canteen quickly passed their goal of $7,500 by almost $2,200.

The Troy Foundation immediately stepped up with a donation of $500.

On March 31, the Canteen expenses were $881.12 and cash was needed if the Canteen was to continue. Some five thousand solicitation letters were mailed, seeking donations. A goal of $7,500 was announced on March 27, and within one day donations were pouring in. In the first four days of the campaign $3,470 was received. The Citizens Service Committee sent $500 and the Miami County Chapter of the American Red Cross made a donation of $200. By April 17, over $9,000 had been received and donations were still pouring in. Mrs. Tooley began sending each donor a personal acknowledgment card.

The final report of the fund raising campaign found 1,284 donors contributing $9,660.28. In addition she reminded everyone they needed more magazines, games, books, puzzles and playing cards.

The girls had begun extending their work as a result of seeing many Hospital Trains of wounded soldiers passing through. While the girls weren't allowed on the trains, through the windows they saw the many wounded. There were boys with their heads heavily bandaged, amputees, boys carrying the blank stares of battle shock, those who were deaf and other life-altering injuries. Quietly they began making up gift boxes for the hospitals where these soldiers were going, packed with cookies, games, playing cards, books and magazines.

These very young ambassadors and their adult supervisors were also the witnesses to the price of freedom. They were greeting the heroes of global conflict. The girls had seen tens of thousands of soldiers; recruits, those fresh from basic training, veterans, and the wounded. Everyone got a smile. They all stood and waved as the cars of each train passed them on the long journey.

The ladies rule of thumb in making up bags of food was for three bags to each coach. In the first ten months of operation it amounted to approximately 12,500 bags of food. This was no small task.

From the time the canteen started until the end of March 1945, the girls made up all the bags and baskets in the Canteen at Union Street Park. They carried them over or wheeled them over in a three-wheel cart to the station platform. They endured terrible heat, rain storms and the worst winter weather in over 100 years. It had not gone unnoticed. Mrs. Hartzell, who herself was a regular volunteer, saw to the acquisition of an enclosed trailer and an old Model T truck with which to pull it. The trailer was a greatly appreciated addition since it allowed the girls to work more efficiently at the station platform. It was equipped with shelves, a small heating stove and a counter across dutch doors. An awning could be set over the counter area to afford better protection. Fresh food, drinks and magazines were served to many from the counter. In addition it carried those many baskets and bags of food. The trailer also gave the girls an opportunity to get out of adverse weather.

First thing every day, the ladies would get the food ready and load it into the trailer for the morning trains. Mary Tooley drove it across the tracks and parked it near the north end of the station platform. The morning trains were serviced without the need to run back and forth between the canteen and the railroad. It was taken back over after lunch and resupplied for the afternoon and evening trains. Ruth McWilliams manned the trailer's compact kitchen and made sandwiches there as needed. Mary used the truck to pick up pies at the Blue Bird bakery, bread from grocers and other needed supplies. Gasoline for the truck was allotted by the government as a necessary service.

The surrender of Germany occurred on May 8, 1945. The news was calmly greeted. There was no vociferous celebration. The local stores closed to observe a holiday and permit the people to attend services in many of the local churches. A national day of prayer was observed. Most churches in Troy held formal services that evening to thank God for an end to the war in Europe, for the safety of the troops and for the surrender of Japan.

Allied soldiers in Germany took on the roles of care workers, security guards, utility workers and interim local government leaders in many of the bombed-out towns. Back here the home folks were requested to take on an equal task.

While the Junior Canteen girls were meeting all the trains, Troy, as so many cities across the United States was ask to give any surplus clothing to local service agencies for shipment to Europe.

The war refugees needed clothes, food and other basic needs. Not that the United States hadn't done enough to crush the evil tyranny of a brutal totalitarian regime, the home front took on the task of raiding their personal closets for any clothing that might be suitable for use by the civilians of those defeated countries.

At no other point in world history has the event of spontaneous aid come forth as it did when the good and decent citizens of America stood up again and took care of the peoples of those countries. In Troy, as in many other communities, a used clothing drive was conducted. The donated items were sent to the civilian war victims of Europe. An entire region responded and truck loads of clothes were collected for the unfortunate victims of war on foreign lands.

One very grateful mother in St. Nazaire, France, wrote of her appreciation and thanks to the Red Cross in nearby Allen County. *"I want to thank you very much for the pull-over sweaters which you have sent to me for my two children.*

"I thank the American Red Cross warmly for all it has done for refugees.

"I am very thankful to you." The letter was signed *Madame Heagland.*

As aid landed in a war-torn Europe, many

local soldiers returning from Europe were headed for Camp Atterbury, south of Indianapolis, Indiana, for a furlough and a few were heading home. As quickly as soldiers could be gotten from the battlefield to a seaport, they were put on ships heading for home. The Office of Defense Transportation requested all civilians to refrain from train travel because of the large numbers of military personnel who would be returning to the states. Ports of entry were jam packed with returning soldiers. At times the wait was up to three days for a train to take them west. With Camp Atterbury turned into a military separation center, and troops starting to arrive back from Europe, local soldiers would begin coming home. The Army announced that unless there was a break in the Pacific war front two-thirds of all returning soldiers would be going to invade Japan.

By late May every train coming through Troy, was full of returning soldiers. Many of the men had not enjoyed a glass of fresh cold milk since departing from the States. When they pulled into Troy and saw the girls with their baskets and the canteen trailer, they ran over looking for a glass of fresh milk. It became a priority item to keep on hand. The veterans would promptly down it by the glassful without taking a breath.

A few weeks later school ended for the year and the girls were back at the canteen during the day to greet the rapidly increasing number of troop trains.

On May 21, 1945, at just after 1:00 P.M. a west bound Troop Train derailed at high speed while passing through Piqua, six miles north, on the Pennsylvania Railroad. Twenty-four veterans were injured and over 400 were temporarily stranded. Mary Tooley received an urgent call from the Y.M.C.A. asking for any help the Junior Canteen Girls could give. The derailment was just two blocks west of the Y.M.C.A. facility.

Calls went out in Troy for all the volunteers. The girls and ladies all came. The workers were split because many would be needed in Troy to continue meeting the B & O trains.

About 24 baskets of food were rapidly prepared for the men at Piqua plus additional for trains expected in Troy in less than two hours.

As the girls were to discover when they arrived, most if not all of those men were flyers who had been shot down by the Germans and imprisoned.

A brief article in the Troy paper tells the story of the Junior Girls Canteen efforts that day. *"Sandwiches, coffee, fruit and cookies and volunteers were loaded in automobiles and rushed to the Piqua Y.M.C.A. where the injured and others were taken. These were passed out and were received with pleasure by the battle-scarred veterans of the European conflict gathered there. Many complimentary remarks were heard for the service rendered and many of the boys themselves heaped praise for the thought-*

The West Street Ambassadors

Troop Train wreck at Piqua, May 21, 1945. This view looks southwest on the Pennsylvania Railroad. The Junior Girls Canteen rushed there to serve the soldiers.

This view looks east on the Pennsylvania Railroad. The Y.M.C.A. is to the left and behind the buildings in the center of the picture. That "Y" was the site for the Junior girls Canteen. This was the only time the girls operated from a second site.

Those Last Months of War

Troop Train wreck at Piqua, May 21, 1945. This view of the soldiers was at the Roosevelt Avenue bridge.

Troops unloaded their personal belongings from overturned cars at Piqua, May 21, 1945. The Red Cross was there along with the Junior girls Canteen.

Troop Train wreck at Piqua, May 21, 1945. This view looks east on the Pennsylvania Railroad. Note the WWI veteran acting as a guard on the left. All the uninjured troops walked to the near-by Y.M.C.A. where they were given use of the facilities until another train could be brought in later that evening to take then on to their destinations in Missouri and Texas. -- *All photos collection of author.*

fulness of the act in their behalf."

The number of trains was rapidly increasing throughout the summer as troops came home from Europe to prepare for a possible invasion of Japan.

Mary Tooley was always writing a letter of thanks to some worthy group for a donation. The next week she wrote a letter to the Elks of Troy. *"We would like to thank you for the gifts that you have given to the Junior Girl's Canteen this past year.*

"We find that this Canteen has grown well beyond our fondest dream, and it is only because Troy has such organizations whose interest in the needs of our service people come first.

"May we say that the telephone which you saw fit to install for us soon after it became known what we were trying to do here at the Canteen has been the means of our being able to do the many things for these boys and girls without much notice. Without the telephone and the help of the business men of Troy, we could never begin to supply these soldiers with the things they need to build their morale.

"Your donations have fed many a hungry boy and girl and we at the Canteen want you to know that we are giving fruit to boys who haven't seen an apple, an orange, or a banana in three years. As many of these boys are going on to the South Pacific, we want them to have the feeling that we who stay at home know what they are giving up so that we may have Peace once more."

Every day there were articles in the paper that local boys who had been reported as Missing-In-Action, or had been discovered held in captivity. For others the outcome was the worst news possible. One of the sad realities of working at the canteen were those times when a local boy came home bearing the physical scars of some battle. The girls witnessed those events, along with the arrival of coffins for those who had given their last full measure. They had to focus on their mission of providing a humanitarian service to many others.

The gestures of kindness at this wayside railroad station eased the hurried tenseness and undercurrent that was the tempo of a nation at war. It was a place to glimpse the destinies of the men and women in uniform who had taken the war home to the enemy. These were the people who made up the constantly changing clientele for the canteen girls.

The many soldiers pledged their lives, fortunes and sacred honor to the destruction of evil. They burned their bridges behind them as they underwent the metamorphosis from civilian to service life. With their young lives in front of them, they said good-by to the old routines, and all the trappings of civilian life. They left their jobs, their studies, girl friends, wives and the old gang.

Those were the men who passed by the railroad station and had but the briefest encounter with the canteen volunteers. They stopped only momentarily to enjoy the gracious hospitality and kindness offered them.

They were the battle-scared marines from the South Pacific and places like Saipan, Iwo Jima and Okinawa. Sailors stepped off with tans from working on the ship deck for long hours. Infantry men from the Army who carried a purple heart on a faded uniform from foreign soil were there as were new soldiers, jittery about their coming journey into the yet unknown. Fliers fresh from England who dodged the flack and delivered their deadly packages also alighted from the trains, as did the nurses, lady pilots and others.

Perhaps one soldier stopped on the platform for a moment because the woman pouring coffee reminded him of his mother or one of the girls brought thoughts of his sister or best girl and for a moment the horrors of war were forgotten.

Many times a soldier stopped at the canteen trailer long enough for a sandwich and handed one of the girls a souvenir of a patch or badge from his uniform or that of a German or Jap. Perhaps he thought of his folks back home and grabbed a post card to jot them a quick note. Perhaps passing through his mind were thoughts of his mother baking cookies, just like the one he has in his hand. The smell of warm food and a friendly smile swept him away momentarily. He remembered Skippy, his bedraggled little mutt, basking in the warm sun awaiting his master's return, and of his girl in his arms when the harvest moon was orange and low, and the scent of her hair.

The girls and ladies on the platform could silently salute all these men, for their actions added greatness and the highest value for the glory of the men who were not coming back.

A tiny bit of friendly and warm conversation or a smile from one of the mothers might do much to help them forget terrible experiences of satanic explosions, balls of orange fire, screams and of talking to each other in those horrific

The West Street Ambassadors

moments of making things right with God.

The men who came back from the battlefields, were a mixed toughness and touchiness, impatient with civilian thinking and back-home ways, the indelible stamp of service over seas. They were battle-marked, gaunt, tired, proud of their worn and faded uniforms.

They were the men who just yesterday were the bright-eyed teens who had their hearts full of girl troubles, high school, and jitterbugging at the corner hamburger shop. They grew-up fast! It was very easy the first time a machine gun stuttered their name or they saw the guy laying shoulder to shoulder in a muddy ditch get it.

In a minute or two they stepped back into the coach and disappeared, both the soldiers and the canteen volunteers were changed.

By August, Mary Tooley had announced the Canteen would begin serving all trains including the two night trains, Number 58, due in at 1:56 A.M. and Number 57 due in at 4:40 A.M. The

Canteen Expenses for 1945

March	$ 881.12
April	$ 627.78
May	$ 607.27
June	$ 759.12
July	$1,081.62
August	$1,079.82
September	$1,341.92
October	$ 985.72
November	$ 789.48

neighborhood ladies and their daughters rolled out of bed in the middle of the night to maintain a constant vigil. Some of the girls were allowed to ride their bikes to the canteen in those early hours. They worked very conscientiously with a great deal of zeal, serving weary soldiers and seeing heartbreaking realities of a terrible war.

Troop Trains were running through at all hours. Mary or one of the supervisors would get a call late at night that a Troop Train was on the way. Marleen Reid recalled accompanying her mother for many of those calls. *"Mrs. Tooley would call in the middle of the night and mom would come and get me up. We'd get dressed, go over and get things packed and ready at the canteen. Mrs. Hobbs and her daughter Alice would come over and maybe one or two others, sometimes the Rudisill sisters would be called to help. We met the train and then walked back home, we all lived in the neighborhood."*

Mary had long been doing things to help and support the orphans at the Children's Home near Casstown. She asked the teenage girls if they would like to come and help at the Canteen. One day a week they came and did their part.

Sometimes other neighborhood girls who weren't regular helpers came, and they'd help for a few hours and leave, maybe not coming back for several weeks or even months, it made no matter, every bit of help was appreciated.

Chapter 7

The Troops are Coming Home

August 14, 1945, marked the end of World War II. It was Tuesday. A storm was looming in the west and rain began falling in torrents just after the surrender of Japan was announced at 6:00 P.M.

Less than an hour earlier Mary Tooley learned a 22 car Troop Train was coming south out of Lima. It carried colored troops, many bearing purple hearts and bronze stars from their time on German battlefields. The train stopped in Lima just long enough for a locomotive change but did not stop at that station for canteen services. The men had no knowledge a surrender was about to be announced.

Mary started calling all the volunteers plus other helpers who dropped everything and came quickly to prepare enough food and drinks for the many soldiers. They prepared 20 shopping bags containing sandwiches, 600 pecan pies, hundreds of cookies, 46 decks of playing cards, cigarettes, matches, pencils, post cards and other items.

In the humid August heat, the train crossed the Great Miami River bridge. The troops got glimpses of great crowds of people gathered on the public square as the train crossed Main Street. It came around the curve, easing to a stop south of West Street for water. Most of the

The Troops are Coming Home

At the B & O station platform another group of soldiers are served drinks, sandwiches and given sundry items. In this photo two women in the military are visible in the passenger car vestibule. Mary Tooley, left, pours coffee. -- *Collection of Betty Baldwin*

22 coaches were north of West Street, only a few were at the platform. The veterans were greeted by overwhelming crowds cheering in wild celebration. The men were given the news and invited off for food and drinks.

There were forty girls and adult volunteers on hand with plenty of sandwiches and smiles. One of the volunteers, Doris McMath, recalling that evening said, *"The station grounds were absolutely packed with people awaiting arrival of the train. They were in wild celebration. I think half of Troy must have been there. The station grounds were absolutely packed."*

On the platform was a maximum number of volunteers with food at the ready as joyful shouts of relief suddenly rose from the Canteen. The radio pronounced the long awaited news. The war was over!

An impromptu celebration took place at the platform, on the station grounds and in the park. The troops were given a hero's welcome by thousands of people who came down to the station. They cheered the boys who had helped end the tyranny and set the world on a course of peace. The radio in the Canteen continued to pronounce those sweet words for all to hear.

The whistles of the factories let go. There was a sudden din of car horns and church bells pealed throughout the city. People came out of their homes, danced in the streets, hugged, shot off fireworks and fired guns into the air in celebration. Inside of many homes a prayer of thanks was offered. Churches were opened for prayers and many headed there to kneel in thanksgiving and offer prayers before joining the celebrations.

The men came off the coaches ready to dance. They ate and celebrated right on the platform. A great relief came over the soldiers on that train as they left town. They were headed to Camp Shelby, Mississippi, and a well-earned 30 day

The Troops are Coming Home

furlough. For people in Troy, the celebrations continued for hours. It was difficult at first to know whether to laugh or cry, perhaps a little of both.

Residents had packed the public square. People walked, ran and rode any transportation available to get there. They broke into patriotic songs with a joy in their voices. Even Mother Nature got into the act, letting go with claps of thunder and torrents of rain, but it made little difference. It was well after dark when the crowds finally calmed down.

For the next two days a holiday was observed. In the morning several churches were opened for formal prayer services. All businesses were closed for a two-day holiday.

For the first time in a long time there wasn't any war, it seemed so illusive and at times never-attainable, then in moments, within reach, and so it went for five years. The local fellows went off to war and most came home. A few came home silently, their remains draped in a flag. It was on the same platform at the station.

An hour later, at 7:24 P.M., south bound Number 53 called at the station and crowds cheered and applauded the soldiers who got off for something to eat. Their train had been at the platform in Lima, getting snacks from the canteen ladies when word broke of the surrender of Japan. They witnessed the excitement in that city also.

Across town two days later WACO, who were

building gliders for a planned invasion of Japan, furloughed 750 workers. The government put one of the assembly buildings up for sale, along with many surplus gliders and parts. They had planned to burn the surplus gliders until a local resident offered to buy the inventory. It was all salvaged.

Many Ohio soldiers returning from Europe were headed for Camp Atterbury, south of Indianapolis, for a furlough and a few were heading home. As quickly as soldiers could be gotten from the battlefield to a seaport, they were put on ships heading for home. The Office of Defense Transportation requested all civilians to refrain from train travel because of the large numbers of military personnel who would be returning to the states. With Camp Atterbury turned into a military separation center, and troops starting to arrive back from Europe, local soldiers began coming home.

A lot of these soldiers had been on active duty since early 1942, and many had not seen home since they left. The soldiers, now seasoned veterans, were beginning to appear at the station platform. They came in wearing campaign ribbons, medals, carrying scares, some inward, some exhausted and others needing a boost back. As the trains came, especially at night with the coaches filled to capacity and civilians standing in the aisles or sitting on luggage, there was no really comfortable spot to rest.

Privates, Captains, WACs, WAVEs and sail-

The Troops are Coming Home

ors alike were welcomed by the hospitality of the Canteen girls. This had become a community project and in addition to the regular workers, men and children passed out baskets of sandwiches, cakes, pecan pies, cookies, urns of hot coffee, pitchers of cold milk and lemonade, piles of donuts, stacks of magazines, pencils and post cards. The veterans were greeted like family.

This is the Canteen crew on March 6, 1945. Left to right, Charlene Strome, Phyllis McWilliams, Betty Tooley, Alice Hobbs, Doris McMath, Jeannine Kendall, Nancy Chronaberry, Nanette Rudisill, Eileen Burgin, Helen Turner, Patty Fox, Lois McWilliams, Marilyn Chase, Mary Lou Scott, Rosemary Rudisill, Eleanor Priest, Phyllis Shane, Mary Lee Mumford, Marlene Pour, and Mary Jane Attenweiler. Missing from the photo are; Thelma Dohm, Katherine Hartzell, Kathleen Kendall, Patty Kirkland, Jackie Ovenshire, Mary Margaret Rush, Patricia Ray, Peggy Attenweiler and Hazel Sturgeon. -- *Collection of Betty Baldwin*

Even in the small hours of the morning, volunteers were on hand to graciously and humbly serve the returning soldiers. It was the plain, honest thoughtfulness the veterans appreciated.

The girls saw men come in with beaten-tired expressions on their faces, fresh from a battlefield. Each had played hide-and-seek with death and other trying conditions of war. Perhaps his eyes roamed the station platform, uncertain of this offered hospitality and the smiles of the girls who met them.

The greetings, words of welcome and smiles alone were greatly invigorating. It put a new focus into a well-beaten soul and helped many to catch up with the strangeness of heading home.

Appreciative soldiers began giving the canteen girls rank and company insignias as souvenirs. Several of the girls sewed them to shirts, one to a red flannel shirt, another to an army shirt a GI had given her. They became the uniform at the canteen. Each train brought more soldiers and more patches, some ripping a patch off their uniform on the platform, others tossing them out the windows of the coach. It was their way of saying thanks.

Though it was but a concrete sidewalk along a railroad track, it was Troy's red carpet. Upon that walkway every light and shadow of human existence tread. All the joy, humor and tragedy of man was witnessed there.

The Canteen was being crushed by the surge of returning soldiers. An estimated 275,000 sol-

Division patch of T/5 Walter Danczak. This was the patch of the 5th Infantry Division. It was mailed to the Canteen September 1, 1945, in a gesture of appreciation for the free food. The patch is laying on the letter in which it was enclosed. Hundreds of patches and insignias were given to the Canteen girls as a gesture of appreciation -- *Collection of Betty Baldwin*

diers were fed by the Junior Girls Canteen between May and October 1945.

Meanwhile, Miami Counties' own veteran sons were returning home. Soldiers were discharged from several bases, but a majority came home via Camp Atterbury, Indiana.

Those newly discharged veterans gathered barracks bag, personal items and final transportation papers. Leaving the Camp Atterbury Separation Center, veterans boarded a train on the base for the 30-mile ride north to Indianapolis Union Station and transfer to catch an east bound train to Dayton then north bound to Troy. As the train rolled out the gates and onto the main line of the Pennsylvania Railroad, it was completely strange to feel free from the routines of Army life. In a half hour the train of coaches pulled into the great train shed at Indianapolis Union Station to discharge its newest cargo of newly separated soldiers and enlisted men who were going on furlough. The station was busy with soldiers coming in, heading for Camp Atterbury and others who were departing.

All passengers headed down the stairs and into the concourse of the large brick structure with its massive circular windows, checked the schedule board and arranged transportation papers one last time. Perhaps he visited the USO's Indianapolis Service Canteen in the rear of the station to partake of coffee, sandwiches and doughnuts. Maybe he enjoyed part of the expanse of recreation facilities while awaiting for his train on this long journey. Perhaps he went out onto the streets of Indianapolis, to get some lunch and visit the stores. He may have walked up the street a block or ... to simply stroll along streets that had not been bombed and to savor the fruits of his and many others' labors -- sweet freedom. There was a lack of noise of deuce-and-a-half trucks, tanks, no shell fire or aircraft engines. Perhaps he was listening to the sounds of peace as automobiles plied the streets and people walked about.

Miami county soldiers were usually given a ticket on an eastbound Pennsylvania Railroad train for Dayton, but not always. A few traveled to Sidney on the New York Central Railroad and either phoned home for a ride or transferred to the next south bound B & O train.

As departure time neared the veteran gathered his things, walked back up the stairs to the assigned platform (Indianapolis Union Station is an elevated station), along the trackside platform and boarded the coach. Handing his ticket to the conductor for one last time, he and and and then took a coach seat to await its momentary departure. With two blasts of the whistle the locomotive began to bark its exhausts and the train eased out on this the most important leg of the journey yet. They passed through industrial neighborhoods, passing one last railroad yard before slipping into the country as the train ran at maximum speed. Most soldiers' wives or parents had gotten a call detailing train schedules, but a few surprised their folks or wives.

Every beat of the locomotive exhaust and scream of the whistle was one step closer to his destination. They passed through small towns with familiar names, Greenfield, Knightstown, Cambridge City, Germantown, Centerville and Richmond, Indiana. Pulling from the station they passed through the industrial district of Richmond and along the PRR yards. The train passed Glen Tower and glided east through a gentle valley and across the state line at New Paris, Ohio. At the railroad junction they took the Dayton Branch eastward. The train sped through West Manchester, Brookville, Trotwood and finally the long awaited call... "DAY-TON, next stop Dayton."

It had to be thrilling when the train brakes took hold and it crossed the Great Miami River bridge easing to a stop along the platforms in downtown Dayton. He stood up from the coach seat, walked to the end of the car and grabbed his duffle bag. As the train stopped, he stepped out and down the steps onto the platform and back on good ole Ohio soil. Some of the local soldiers called their wife or parents in the hope they had gas in the car and could come down and get them. Others stayed in Dayton to transfer trains or catch a bus.

As trains neared Troy, soldiers and veterans lined up in the coach vestibule to make the dash to the Canteen trailer. One soldier would perhaps step off the train and head for the station, into the arms of loved ones. As the train stopped, he stood up from the coach seat, walked to the end of the car, grabbed his duffle bag and perhaps peered out the window to see familiar faces. As soon as the train stopped, he stepped out and down the steps and onto the solid soil of Troy,

Insignia of the Honorably Discharged soldier from WW II. This one was worn home by a Miami County soldier in July 1945. -- *Author's collection*

The Troops are Coming Home

This March 1945, photo of the ladies meeting a train of soldiers in the rain. A Large patio umbrella handily protected the food and drinks from the rain. Left to right, the ladies are, Mary Hobbs, Ruth McWilliams, Mary Tooley and May Butler -- *Collection of Betty Baldwin*

Miami County, Ohio.

Moving along the platform he walked, or perhaps half ran through the crowd to a long overdue welcome with his family at the station. There were hugs and kisses, hand shakes and tears of joy as they moved along. Perhaps they walked up to the Canteen trailer to say hello to the girls and women working there, and to let them know another one had made it home safely.

Chapter 8

We Won't Let the Boys Down

As the trainloads of veterans came through, at Troy they were made to feel their victory was appreciated. The faithful staff of teenage girls and the daytime lady volunteers felt the expressions appreciation had to continue on behalf of the grateful people of Troy and the region. Across the United States several canteens had closed their doors by November 1945, for a lack of funds, others closed from overly tired volunteers, and some for a simple lack of interest in the soldiers now coming home in great numbers.

The endeavors of the canteen girls produced a joy of having brought a moment of happiness to some fellows who were just passing through from one service assignment to another or journeying through on leave. The ladies and town residents continued the canteen no matter how tired they were, or how many had come through, even in summer heat or winter's worst cold. Mrs. Tooley was ask whether it was worth it? She replied, *"Maybe we do give up some rest, some well prepared food, and some of our fun. But they continue, if there is a chance that we can keep even one boy from growing bitter, isn't that just what we should do?"*

In late August 1945, one afternoon an extra large troop train stopped at Troy en route to

Camp Campbell, Kentucky. It was none other than General George Patton's Fifth Armored Division, and they were all amply served by that same group of girls. A letter came from one of the troops the next week expressing their appreciation.

"On or about Aug. 23, 1945, a troop train, carrying General Patton's Fifth Division stopped while en route from Camp Devens, Mass., to Camp Campbell, Ky., after having returned from the European theater of operations.

"The unit had travelled thousands of miles through the United States, Iceland, England, Ireland, France, Germany and Czechoslovakia. We thought we had seen about everything. Without warning a number of young women began descending upon our forces bearing enormous paper bags. As they closed in upon us an endless row of these mysterious bags kept pouring through each of the open windows of the long train.

"We looked inside... and found huge quantities of delicious pies, cakes, cookies, and magazines, with a little tag attached extending the best wishes of the Junior Girls Canteen of Troy, O."

They were extended a hearty thanks. Many times when a soldier discovered his money was no good at the canteen, they resorted to giving the girls something else in appreciation. They would tear off an insignia or stripes from their uniform and throw them out of the coach windows as souvenirs. Mary Chase began sewing hers to a red flannel shirt and wearing it on the days she worked at the Canteen. By the time the Canteen closed she had amassed an amazing collection that included insignias, ribbons, medals and a pair of German Air Force Wings.

With the start of the 1945 school year the Canteen girls were making plans for the fall and winter seasons. They had expanded their focus and were also sending boxes of items to many of the general hospitals and military hospitals treating all the veterans. They had gotten into collecting records albums around town and sent them to those places.

The girls, at their monthly meeting for September, asked that the magazine room be turned into a study area so that they might do their homework while staffing the canteen.

As the last months of 1945 melted away, a letter came to the canteen from a Major on behalf of his troops.

November 8, 1945
Fort Devens, Mass.

Dear Members:

I wish to express my deep appreciation and heartfelt thanks to you all for your generosity and expressions of thanks to us veterans from overseas by your distribution of food and magazines to us upon our train stopover at your local railway station Nov. 7.

The men expressed themselves as deeply grateful to you all, not only for the material gifts but also for your thoughtfulness. The men feel that at least some folks at home have not forgotten them. Again sincerest thanks, not only for myself but all the soldiers on that train.

Major John Olsovsky

Another letter was equally powerful in expressing appreciation for food and gifts given to the veteran troops at Troy by the canteen girls.

November 9, 1945

Dear Girls:

The nicest gesture I have ever had the pleasure to be the recipient of happened as I sat in a grimy day coach, stopped for a few minutes in Troy, Ohio, on Nov, 9, 1945.

The purpose of this letter is to tell you just how much all of us appreciated and enjoyed the delicious cakes and cookies which you so generously gave.

Everything occurred so quickly that none of us knew exactly what was happening. I don't believe the train stopped more than three minutes, but in that time maga-

zines and all those good things to eat appeared miraculously.

I don't believe that you know that the train was filled with men from New England, and as you perhaps have heard we New Englanders are a rather conservative and reticent lot.

Well-- as the train moved along out of Troy, Ohio, and everyone realized what had happened, we looked at one another and didn't say a word. We all knew that the United States was all that we thought it was -- and it took you and Troy, Ohio to convince us.

All the men feel as I do, and because of that this letter is written to express our sincere thanks and admiration for the work you are doing.

Lt. D. P. Dineen
35th Ind. Div.

Many veterans felt their homecoming from the battle front was a letdown. They felt that those at home did not understand their experiences in war. Such was not the case at Troy in the months following the surrender of Japan. The soldiers were not numbers, the girls on the platform were ambassadors for an entire region who cared enough to continue making the gestures of food, gifts and magazines for those many strangers. It was with a great deal of appreciation for all the soldiers that all the trains were met and all the soldiers were fed and acknowledged.

Through November and December 1945, The girls met all the trains. The Canteen continued on with plenty of work yet to be done; food and smiles were the order for returning soldiers. The hospitality continued for another month with a new mission of providing a welcome to returning veterans.

With volunteers pressed to serve the tremendous volume of redeployed and discharged personnel, supporters continued to respond with food and cash in grateful appreciation for their duty to the cause of liberty and freedom.

There was however one significant problem that cropped up during the holiday season 1945 - a lack of volunteers. Many veterans from the Miami County region were home. Mothers, wives and sisters wanted to spend time with their loved-ones and schedules of workers became hard to fill. Not helping the matter, another cold snap hit the region about December 14, and ran through Christmas with temperatures hovering between six-below-zero and four above.

During the week before Christmas, the number of soldiers coming into Troy daily was rapidly rising and a few hundred a day were quickly rising to over a thousand daily. Trains were filled to capacity. The railroad had to send part of its passenger equipment west to help move returning soldiers from the Asia-Pacific The-

The West Street Ambassadors

ater back home. In the immediate days before Christmas as trains stopped, there was almost no room to take on waiting passengers. Coach aisles, and even vestibules were packed full of people and large numbers of soldiers trying to get home.

January 1946, opened with the girls meeting the trains. They made a public appeal for magazine and playing cards. Without sufficient volunteers the girls were not able to serve hot chocolate and coffee and the food items were limited to pecan pies and cookies. The time for continued operation of the canteen was becoming quite limited.

At a noon potluck lunch, on January 6, the canteen directors decided to continue one week at a time until funds and supplies were exhausted. Finally on Friday, February 1, in a small article in the *Troy Daily News*, it was announced the canteen would serve its final trains the next day. *"The Junior Girls Canteen, through its director, Mrs. Mary Tooley, announced Friday that the work which the organization has conducted almost three years in servicing the troop trains as they passed through Troy carrying soldiers to the various camps and then returning them to their homes after the close of WWII, will be brought to a close Saturday. The wholehearted work of this group has attracted nationwide attention and was also extended to foreign lands.*

"The travel of the service men and women has

slowed down the last week to the extent that this action was warranted, Mrs. Tooley stated."

The next day north bound Number 54, scheduled for 2:50 PM arrival at Troy. As it arrived, a Conductor announced "Troy, Troy, next stop."

On the platform Canteen volunteers grouped around the serving cart. They were several of the Canteen supervisors, several of the girls along with Mary Tooley.

A group of new recruits is afforded food, drinks, magazines and sundry items on the platform of the B & O at Troy. This March 1945 photo is testimony to the dedication of the ladies. Left to right, the ladies are, Miriam Hartzell, May Butler, soldier, Ruth McWilliams and Mary Hobbs. -- *Collection of Betty Baldwin*

The West Street Ambassadors

The train eased to a stop and soldiers hopped off to take magazines and cookies.

While the men boarded the train, up at the locomotive the train's fireman swung the water spout away and climbed over the coal pile for the warmth of the engine cab. The soldiers disappeared into the coaches with the snacks while offering their expressions of appreciation.

The conductor snapped the trap door closed. With two whistle blasts the train pulled out. The ladies waved to the men in the passing coaches. Mary Tooley, her friends and some of the girls walked across the park in the cold of that February afternoon. Perhaps thinking about all the good the girls had done in almost three years of constant service and the hundreds of thousands of faces of those many soldiers. Their work was not quite finished.

On Thursday, February 7, an all-day meeting of the canteen staff was held, it included a luncheon. The ladies came to clean up the canteen structure and work on their hospital gift boxes.

They continued packing gift boxes for four more months, sending them to many hospitals for the wounded veterans.

The last train on February 2, was not to be the last train. Throughout February, Troop Trains rolled into town and every day that one came there were two or three ladies on the platform with magazines, cookies and on two occasions, ice cream and soda pop.

By the last of February it looked as though a

final end was in sight as fewer trains came and there were less returning veterans and less recruits headed for basic training.

On March 10, 1946, one last south bound Troop Train came in, headed south for Keesler Field Biloxi, Mississippi. The ladies met the recruits with their usual fare of magazines and cookies. When the locomotive finished taking on water the engineer sounded two short blasted and headed south, whistling for Union Street crossing, then the train rapidly disappeared from sight. The ladies walked across the tracks for the last time, their long vigil as Troy's West Street Ambassadors was finally over.

The canteen ended quietly and the girls continued their schooling. Unlike the other canteens in Ohio, in Troy there was no public testimonial for the girls and their mothers. Mrs. Hartzell and a few of the ladies took the girls to Cincinnati's Coney Island for a day that next summer. They had the memories of three endearing years during their teens to reflect on, a few letters some pen-pals and a few token souvenirs. The City of Troy removed the temporary exterior walls from the Canteen and returned it to a picnic shelter. It was demolished in the 1970s. In 1971, passenger service ended on the B & O and the concrete platform was removed.

Chapter 9

The Flowers are From Tennessee

Letters of appreciation poured in from all over the world—from G.I.s to Generals—saying, "Thanks! God bless you! Keep up the good work!"

On March 4, 1945, a group of soldiers heading to Keesler Field, Mississippi, stopped in Troy. They were moving from Fort Devens, Massachusetts, and had been on the train about three days. They were given snacks, games and magazines. Their thoughtful letter was signed by 19 very appreciative soldiers who enclosed wild flowers from Tennessee.

"Dear Girls:

"This is a note of thanks for the candy, cards and magazines that you gave to our troop train that passed through Troy March 4.

"We had just had chow that my dog wouldn't have eaten, and that candy was a present from heaven. Thanks again and keep up the good work.

"P.S. That's the only town that gave us more than a grin. Please excuse the writing, just blame it on the train."

"Sincerely yours,
Ed, Joseph B. Addante Jr. (The one who wanted to kiss the little sweet master sargent),

The Flowers are From Tennessee

Walter E. Allard Jr. (God Bless all of you), Johnny Becker (And Sarge, it was me, not Joe), Howard Allen, (The Green Mountain Kid), et al."

These are the actual flowers from Tennessee. One group of soldiers enclosed with their letter of appreciation - wild flowers from the Tennessee Mountains. Their train was stopped along the railroad when one of the soldiers hopped off and plucked some wild flowers, a thoughtful gesture for the Canteen girls. The photo above reveals the small note and the dried flowers, 61 years after they were sent. Among the many letters that soldiers sent, some contained money others had patches and some had foreign currency or souvenirs. Of the thousands of letters from various canteens the author has read, this is the only one to mention flowers. -- *Photo by Author, Collection of Betty Baldwin*

From a former Troy fellow, Pfc. Herbert R. Hill he wrote his feelings about how the canteen was helping the soldiers. His letter was mailed from Cincinnati June 26, 1945.

"Last week - June 20 to be exact - the train on which I was traveling to visit my 82-year-old grandmother in Fletcher, stopped at the Troy station for about seven minutes. While there I hopped off to take advantage of your canteen service - a practice which has been mine in my army travels all over the country- (and I'm sure the habitual practice of all GIs everywhere) for 14 months. I can't understand why I do this unless there's some unexplainable mysterious allure you pretty girls with your canteens hold for us in the army. Anyhow, I wasn't even hungry at 10 o'clock in the morning, but still, following some GI instinct, I played the hunch and went to see what you were offering.

What I really wanted was a box of matches so I could light my pipe. I had left my own at home - forgotten them - and hadn't had a smoke all the way from Cincinnati. You'd be surprised how a few draws from a well broken in pipe alleviates a man's loneliness. To my amazement you really did have matches. I felt so thankful I forgot to be lonely to the conclusion of my journey that day, and even took some candy, a pecan pie and chewing gum.

I want to thank you for your excellent canteen

service and to compliment you too. You have the finest canteen of its type I've met up with yet, that is, for the size of towns like Troy. I hope you continue the good work, even if you can't possibly know how much you will be appreciated or thanked, for you see, not every soldier will take the time to write you. But services like yours will long be remembered after the war is over for the unpleasantries of life have a tendency to be forgotten, and the pleasantries remembered.

I shall not only remember you always, but with cherished pride, because, you see, I count Troy my home town, having come there to live when I was three years old and stayed until I was ten. I used to live at 334 Garfield Avenue, and attended Kyle and Edwards schools. I owned a bicycle, had a paper route and played with boys and girls of Troy almost your age (maybe not quite).

Again, it was nice to come back to one's home town if only to spend a brief five or ten minutes, and have girls like you fill the needs of my heart- and body - just perfectly.

God Bless America!

Pfc Herbert R. Hill

Another letter came from a sailor in Florida. His letter was typical of the type many canteens received.

"Dear Girls:

"I am writing this letter to thank you and show my appreciation for the kindness shown us fellows as we passed through your little town last Sunday. Believe me when I say that yours is the only club of any city that we passed through on an 1,800 mile trip that showed us any hospitality. We were glad to get the pies and more than overjoyed to get the playing cards. I will never forget the way we were treated in Troy and I'm sure the other fellows won't either.

"A Sailor in Pensacola, Fla."

A V-Mail letter came all the way from France in November 1944, with an amusing situation noted.

"Just a note of appreciation for the swell reception and food that we received when our train passed through your city recently. It so happened our stove broke down that noon and as a result we had little dinner till we hit Troy. I assure you the fellows appreciated it.
"Signed by soldiers from Michigan, Minnesota, Tennessee, Wisconsin, Arizona, Texas, New York and New Jersey."

On February 22, 1946, a simple post card arrived with a very familiar signature.

The Flowers are From Tennessee

"Dear Girls,

"We would like to express our sincere appreciation for the generous gifts that you have so kindly given us as we passed through your town. It warmed our hearts to see that there are people who still remember the boys in service.

"Very Truly Yours,
"G. I. Joe"

On April 25, 1945, came a note with typical expressions of appreciation and a mention of the cash situation for many of the soldiers. Many who were traveling home had just enough money for a ticket and almost nothing left for food, so the canteen was an oasis.

"Just a note of thanks for the grand cookies I got on my trip home. I live in Birmingham, Alabama."

"Gosh, I ran out of money. I only had my ticket and 20 cents in my pocket. I saw the ladies when the train stopped. I flew off with my 20 cents in my hand. The Conductor called me back. 'These ladies said No Charges, soldier.'

"Gosh, I didn't even have time to thank her for the cookies and coffee. But I'll just say thanks a million to all the members.

"Very Sincerely,
Pfc Wm. B. Herring"

The West Street Ambassadors

The Roster of Identified Volunteers

MOTHERS AND NEIGHBORS
Ellen Abshire
Sarah Attenweiler
May Butler
Elizabeth Galbreath
Miriam Hartzell
Mary Hobbs
Mrs. R. Kinder
Ruth McWilliams
Loretta Pour
Mrs. Frank Renneker
Mrs. Robbins
Opal Scott
Mary O'Connell-Sundrup
Mary Tooley
Margaret Wilt

THE CANTEEN GIRLS
Mary Jane Attenweiler
Peggy Attenweiler
Eileen Burgin
Marilyn Chase
Nancy Chronaberry
Thelma Dohm
Patty Fox
Katherine Hartzell
Alice Hobbs
Jeannine Kendall
Kathleen Kendall
Patty Kirkland
Doris McMath
Lois McWilliams
Phyllis McWilliams
Mary Lee Mumford
Jackie Ovenshire
Eleanor Priest
Marlene Pour
Patricia Ray
Nanette Rudisill
Rosemary Rudisill
Mary Margaret Rush
Mary Lou Scott
Phyllis Shane
Charlene Strome
Hazel Sturgeon
Betty Tooley
Helen Turner

MASCOT
Mickey Attenweiler

Canteen Advisory Committee

Mrs. Mary Tooley, President
Mrs. Ruth McWilliams, Vice President
Mrs. Miriam Hartzell, Secretary
Herbert Ross, Treasurer
Mrs. Noble Wilt
Reverend A. M. Dixon
Coleman Scott
Cameron Dungan

Community Fund Drive Chairman
James Mischler

The West Street Ambassadors

Identified Organizations Supporting the Canteen

Mayflower Theatre
Montgomery Ward & Company
Montross Lumber Company
Howard Mouch Furniture
Neal's Dairy
Miami County Dairy
Oxley's Drug Store
Pearson's Laundry & Dry Cleaning
J. C. Penney Company
Ruby's Beauty Salon
Schnell's Plumbing & Heating
John Shanesy Store
Steil-Grunder Dye Company
Strock Clothing
Tip Top Canning
Tip-Top Potato Chips
Blue Bird Baking Company
American Legion
Veterans of Foreign Wars
Elks Lodge
Eagles Lodge
Kiwanis Club, Troy, Ohio
Dewey's Grocery
Hartzell Hardwoods
The Troy Foundation
Citizens Service Committee
Miami County Chapter American Red Cross
Troy Country Club
Fletcher Community Grange
American War Dads
VanCleve School
Heywood School
Kyle School

Edwards School
Troy Sunshade
Gummed Products Company
Christian Class 7
Hobart Brothers Company
Lamda Chi Omega Soroity
W. H. Hobart Sr.
Charles Trostel
Hobart Manufacturing Company
Browers Stationers
National Biscuit Company
Mayor J. D. Boak, Troy
City Transfer Company
Y.M.C.A. at Piqua
Waco Aircraft Company
City of Troy
Fletcher Community Grange
Mr. & Mrs. Robert N. Hartzell
Mr. & Mrs. Murlon Isenbarger
Mr. Paul Herrlinger
Aeroproducts Division, General Motors
District 7, Ohio Deptartment of Highways
Peoples Building & Savings Association
Several Church Groups (not otherwise identified)

NOTE: There were 1,248 unidentified individual donors to the Canteen in April 1945.

Gift Boxes prepared by the Canteen for Veterans Hospitals

Nichols General Hospital, Louisville, Kentucky
Fletcher General Hospital, Cambridge, Ohio
V.A. Hospital, Dayton, Ohio
Crile General Hospital, Cleveland, Ohio
Ashford General Hospital,
         White Sulphur Springs, West Virginia
Woodrow Wilson General Hospital, Stanton, Virginia
V.A. Hospital, Tucson, Arizona
Billings General Hospital,
         Fort Benjamin Harrison, Indiana
Percy Jones Hospital, Fort Custer, Michigan
U.S. Naval Hospital, Camp LJeune, North Carolina

Bibliography

Piqua Daily Call 1944 and 1945
Troy Daily News 1944 and 1945
Miami Union 1944 and 1945
The Lima News 1944 and 1945
Dayton Daily News 1945

Letters from soldiers, et al served at the Canteen, collection of Betty Baldwin.

Photographs of the Junior Girls Canteen, collection of Betty Baldwin.

Interviews with Canteen volunteers and families conducted during April and May 2006 by the author.

Timetables of the Baltimore & Ohio Railroad 1943 - 1946.

Sanborn Fire Insurance map of Troy, Ohio 1930 - 1940.

Unspecified articles on the Canteens at Springfield, Ohio and Lima, Ohio.

Bombing records of USAAF on file at Rutgers University.

The Columbus Avenue Miracle © 2005, Scott D. Trostel, Cam-Tech Publishing, P. O. Box 341, Fletcher, Ohio 45326-0341

The Lima's Operation Kindness © 2006, Scott D. Trostel, Cam-Tech Publishing, P. O. Box 341, Fletcher, Ohio 45326-0341

Read More Uplifting Stories About the WW II Canteens...

THE COLUMBUS AVENUE MIRACLE At Bellefontaine, Ohio, wives of railroad men provided free lunch to every soldier passing through town on the New York Central Railroad. For 45 months around the clock, over 700,000 soldiers were nourished with donated food served by unpaid volunteers on the station platforms.
The volunteer canteen workers' showed incredible spirit and selfless sacrifice. This became the rallying point for the community. Ladies all over town and in the rural areas made baked goods; pies, cakes, cookies and cooked food without hesitation. Sandwiches were made by the basket full. Sunday school classes, high school and grade school classes, ladies clubs, grange members, farmers, even groups of employees from local merchants and manufacturers stepped forward to help in any way they could. They knew it was the men and women in uniform who were making the greater sacrifice. From 1942 to 1946, they served soldiers passing through on furlough, troop trains, hospital trains, and even the P.O.W. trains were humbly served.
ISBN 0-925436-50-X • 176 pages • 5 1/2 x 8 1/2 • Soft cover $11.95

LIMA'S OPERATION KINDNESS Lima, Ohio's, inspiring story of hundreds of dedicated volunteers who fed over four million soldiers and sailors at Lima's railroad stations during WW II, Korea and Viet Nam Wars. This was the longest operating railroad canteen in the United States.
This is a moving portrayal of devoted and selfless giving. Soldiers derived a powerful sense of purpose when greeted with friendly smiles and words of encouragement.
Volunteers greeted thousands of troops daily. They served at track side, overcoming significant difficulties. Supported by donations from eleven counties, they did not allow the supply of scarce items to fail.
The text is laced with stirring letters from appreciative service men and women. Lima's dedicated track side ambassadors of kindness waved good-byes to those headed to battle and offered thanks to veterans who stood in defense of freedom and liberty from 1942 until 1970. It was Lima's finest hour!
ISBN 0-925436-51-8 • 130 pages • 8 1/2 x 11 • Soft cover $26.95

Available from *Cam-Tech Publishing*
                       P.O. Box 341
                       Fletcher, Ohio 45326-0341

Add $2.50 shipping for the first book and $.50 for each additional book.